MW00629281

Military Recruiting

Strategies & Tactics

After several years of struggling to make our recruiting goals, we swapped our former sales model for the IMPACT Selling® System in early 2000. What followed is simply remarkable. Armed with an applicant-focused approach to presenting our recruiting opportunities, Air Force Reserve Command Recruiting Service has surpassed its mission requirements nine straight years. Just as importantly, a significantly higher number of our recruiters have found success and satisfaction in being part of the military recruiting profession. With the publication of Military Recruiting Strategies and Tactics, Kevin Reinert and Bill Brooks have delivered a practical and powerful tool for recruiters everywhere, regardless of the service they represent.

Francis M. Mungavin, Colonel, USAF (Retired)
Former Commander, Air Force Reserve Command Recruiting Service

When the Air National Guard converted to the IMPACT Selling® System in 2007, we not only upgraded to a new sales model that has worked magnificently, we also gained a valued partner at The Brooks Group. Kevin Reinert masterfully guided us through a myriad of challenges as we trained more than 500 men and women – and all at the same time. I was thrilled to hear that Kevin has combined his military recruiting experience with the decades of professional sales research of Bill Brooks to author Military Recruiting Strategies and Tactics. It's a much-needed text that details the unique challenges military recruiters encounter every single day, and it offers the right solutions to guarantee long-lasting professional success and satisfaction.

Randy D. Johnson, Lt Col, USAF (Retired)
Former Director, ANG Recruiting and Retention Division

Military Recruiting Strategies and Tactics is a fabulous reference tool for rookie recruiters and seasoned 'bag carriers.' Kevin Reinert and Bill Brooks clearly remind readers that military recruiting is selling, and in today's complex recruiting marketplace, 'old school' manipulative techniques simply don't work anymore. Together, Bill and Kevin share a lifetime of selling and military recruiting experience and provide dozens of illustrations and ideas recruiters can apply every day of their careers. I only wish the book was written years ago so I could have given a copy to all of my recruiting school students.

Marcus Schachle, SMSgt, USAF (Retired)
Former Instructor Supervisor, US Air Force Recruiting School

This book is a prescription for success for any military recruiter. Colonel Reinert has meticulously compiled all the strategies, tactics, and techniques that made him one of the United States Air Force's top recruiting officers. What makes this literary work special is the writer was not just a manager who told his recruiters "to do as I say" but a leader who showed them how "to do as I do." Kevin was a real 'bag carrier.' He carried a goal, knew how to make his goal, and that's why our squadron was successful. This is an excellent read – one that recruiters should keep handy for future reference.

Daniel K. Duffey, Lt Col, USAF (Retired)
Former Air Force Recruiting Squadron Commander

Colonel Reinert, 'the officer,' and Mr. Brooks, 'the gentleman,' have perfectly penned a guide to success every recruiter can and should follow. Military Recruiting Strategies and Tactics is a "no punches pulled" textbook that smartly communicates an approach to military recruiting with the aim of perpetuating the prestige and respect future servicemembers deserve. The book is a must read for current recruiting professionals or anyone considering a tour of duty (or career) in military recruiting.

Brian K. Yoh, Principal at BKY LLC, PMP
Former Air Force Reserve Command Senior Recruiter & Recruiting Officer

Military Recruiting
Strategies & Tactics

Kevin Reinert, Colonel, USAF (Retired)
and William T. Brooks

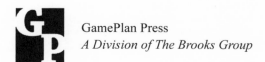

GamePlan Press
A Division of The Brooks Group

Copyright © 2010 by William T. Brooks and GamePlan Press. All Rights Reserved.

No part of this book may be reproduced or utilized in any form or by any means, electronic or mechanical, including photocopying, recording, or by any information storage and retrieval system, without permission in writing from the publisher.

GamePlan Press
A Division of The Brooks Group
3810 N Elm Street, Suite 202
Greensboro, NC 27455

www.thebrooksgroup.com | 800.633.7762

Contents

Preface

Since our emergence as an independent nation in 1776, Americans have preferred to shy away from maintaining large-standing armed forces. In fact, for the vast majority of our first 200 years of existence, the United States employed a combination of volunteerism and conscription to provide for the nation's defense, with the latter approach mostly exercised when the threat of war was imminent. To a great degree, the strategy was successful, particularly during the first half of the 20th Century, when the United States soundly defeated its enemies in two World Wars. By the time the Germans and Japanese surrendered in 1945, our 'citizen soldiers' were anxious to return home to their families and pre-war careers. Life would go on as before, only better, now that the world was safe for democracy.

However, by 1948, the United States found itself on the brink of nuclear holocaust with the Soviet Union. Nicknamed the *Cold War*, the political differences sometimes turned hot. Conflict broke out in Korea in 1950, and in the 1960s, America sent millions of its sons (and some daughters) to Vietnam to stem the spread of Communism.

Despite noble intentions, America's failure to successfully prosecute the Vietnam War, combined with the deaths of more than 58,000 American troops, divided its citizens in ways not seen since the Civil War. Furthermore, President Lyndon Johnson's decision not to mobilize significant numbers of reserve component forces, coupled with a military draft perceived by many as unfair to the lower economic strata of American society, decreased American military capability and eroded public support for the war.

In 1973, as America withdrew its forces from Vietnam, President Richard Nixon oversaw two critical initiatives that would eventually have long-reaching positive effects on the United States military. First, he ended the military draft. Henceforth, America would fill the ranks of its armed forces only with volunteers. Second, the Department of Defense implemented the Total Force Policy that called for higher levels of readiness in the reserve components and a decree that reserve forces would be integrated on an operational level with their active duty counterparts.

Today, as America faces serious threats from terrorists, the performance of our servicemembers has never been better, and the contributions of the reserve components, though greatly stretched, have been remarkable. And often overlooked, but nevertheless vital, have been the roles played by the armed services' recruiting teams.

The men and women working in military recruiting organizations represent the tip of the military spear. As recruiters, they are the conduit by which virtually all new recruits enter military service. And while there are thousands of military recruiters, not everyone who takes on those duties finds success year after year.

This book could help you join the ranks of the great recruiters who experience personal satisfaction and reap professional rewards. But whether that happens is totally up to you. As you'll discover, recruiting is a science that when practiced correctly becomes an art form. Make no mistake about it... when we talk about recruiting, we're also talking about selling. Many of your prospects will never understand the value of a military commitment unless you, as their recruiter, can accurately explain its value and persuade each person that joining the military is a great opportunity. That, by nature, is what professional selling (recruiting) is all about.

Here's the real truth about your career field. Successful recruiters study their profession, train diligently and work hard. How hard are you willing to work? We assure you that no strategy or tactic in this book will work unless you do. Consequently, the challenge is now yours.

Why Read This Book?

Whether you're a rookie recruiter or a seasoned professional, there are strategies and tactics in this book to help propel your career to the next level.

The contents have been honed through more than 30 years of sales and recruiting, sales and recruiting management, training and coaching experience with hundreds of thousands of sales and recruiting professionals worldwide.

Whether you recruit enlisted personnel or officer candidates, prior-service or non-prior service applicants, medical or line officers, or for active-duty or reserve components, there are hundreds of invaluable ideas in this book.

Knowledge is valuable, and action is equally important. Don't read the suggestions in this book and then just think about them – apply them in your daily activities. Ideas that stay within the pages of a book are worthless. The recruiting strategies and tactics you'll read about must be tested, modified, adapted or changed, as needed, to fit your unique recruiting environment.

Overview of the Book

The first chapter welcomes you to the world of contemporary military recruiting and describes what the profession is all about. Find out about the biggest challenges facing today's military recruiters. Learn the two biggest mistakes that could derail your recruiting career, followed by the twenty biggest errors to avoid. Discover the Seven Universal Recruiting Rules to guide your career.

Chapter 2 reveals the recruiting profession's most important success secret. Find out how to identify qualified prospects, master the power of understood needs and discover the big difference between being trusted and simply being liked. Read about the authority and ability to commit, sense of urgency, positioning, timing and the six principles that can steer your recruiting career to greater success. You will also learn about the powerful IMPACT Selling® System.

Chapter 3 positions you to better understand the power of focus and how to clarify it. Learn to develop your recruiting philosophy and how to leverage your time, talent, resources and advantage. You'll also have the opportunity to audit your personal recruiting talent.

In Chapter 4, you'll master the power of personal positioning. Learn ten ways to position yourself more effectively with your prospects, applicants and influencers and the six ways you can misposition yourself, along with how to avoid those fatal six mistakes. Discover how to posture yourself as an expert and get tips for dress, style and image as we discuss the powerful role your self-image plays in a recruiting career.

Chapter 5 explains how to differentiate suspects from qualified prospects. Find out how to delve into niches and segments to better enable you to understand your target markets. Learn to use powerful qualifying questions, how to maximize your opportunities for success, how to stay organized, the six things you need to know about your prospects, and much, much more.

Chapter 6 is all about pre-call planning, one of the most overlooked and misunderstood areas in recruiting. Learn the best ways to research your prospects, develop internal support, review your resources and complete your pre-call checklist. Become skilled at mentally and physically preparing yourself for every interview. Discover how to confirm opportunities and guarantee you are ready for every recruiting presentation.

Chapter 7 focuses on how to engage your applicants face-to-face. Learn how to build trust and rapport and ensure you meet every applicant on equal footing. Find out how to reduce tension, be a good host or guest and move smoothly and easily into your recruiting interview. Discover how to transition to the heart of your presentation in a way that guarantees your prospect will be comfortable with you and mentally prepared to listen.

In Chapter 8, you'll learn the power of questions that earn the accession. Gain knowledge of the fatal flaw in recruiting and how to avoid falling into its trap. Find out how to become a better listener. Become skilled at the nine things to avoid when asking questions. Discover dozens of questions you can ask your prospects and applicants, no matter what programs or service you recruit for. Furthermore, this chapter also provides you with the simple, yet most powerful word recruiters can ever use.

Chapter 9 instructs you how to present your recommendations in ways that address your applicant's greatest needs, wants or desires. Learn what value really is and how you can deliver it all the time. Among other things, find out how to avoid commitment issues, stress the right benefits and when to present the commitment. You'll also become skilled at deflecting the age-old "The commitment is too big" objection. You must convince your applicants that your recruiting opportunity is their best option.

In Chapter 10, learn exactly how to do this in unique ways. It's as simple as this: if your applicants don't believe what you tell them, they won't commit! Find out how to ensure your applicants will believe and act on everything you say.

In recruiting, if you can't finalize transactions, you'll fail. It's that basic. In Chapter 11, you'll be taught proven and simple ways to gain the commitment – and how to do it in ways that are not heavy-handed, manipulative or lacking in integrity.

Sustaining self-motivation and momentum is truly an inside job. Nobody else can make that happen for you. The twelfth chapter reveals 10 powerful ways you can stay at the top of your profession for as long as you are a recruiter.

Special Features

The chapters in this book are relatively short, deal with strategic and tactical issues and include many examples. They also feature numerous sidebars designed to give you different types of useful information.

Here's a description of the boxes you'll find in this book.

Good Planning
Tips and tactics for using the ideas in this book to intelligently manage the recruiting process.

Illustration
Examples showing how the principles in the book are applied.

Mine Field
Warnings about where things could go wrong.

Arsenal
Specific procedures to take advantage of the book's advice.

Force Multipliers
How-to and insider hints for techniques to create mutually beneficial relationships.

Threat Reduction
Practical advice on how to minimize the possibility of an error.

Jargon
Every subject has some special terminology. These boxes provide definitions.

Acknowledgements

This book would not be possible without the help of some very special people. Bill Brooks knew more about selling and recruiting than anyone I ever met. Not only was he an expert on the subject, he genuinely cared about the people who earn their living as professional salespeople or military recruiters. It was my privilege and good fortune to meet Bill Brooks during a critical time in my military career. In 1999, I was the Director of Operations and Training for the Air Force Reserve Recruiting Squadron (later called Recruiting Service), and our recruiting efforts were in a four-year downward spiral. Bill Brooks showed me how our recruiting opportunities were powerful, and if presented the right way to our applicants, there was no limit to what our recruiting force could achieve. In 2000, Bill Brooks taught our recruiters the IMPACT Selling® System, and the rest is history. The Air Force Reserve's record of recruiting success since then is truly remarkable.

Many other individuals contributed to my success as a recruiting officer and to the writing of this book.

Lt Col Dan Duffey, USAF (Ret), my first supervisor during my active duty recruiting days, taught me to "Stir the pot" and never to accept the status quo.

Colonel Mike Mungavin, USAF (Ret), was the commander of Air Force Reserve Command Recruiting Service from 2001 to 2008. His brilliant leadership inspired unprecedented recruiting success, and his mentoring efforts on my behalf prepared me to become the Air Force Reserve Command Director of Public Affairs.

I must also recognize every recruiter who ever "carried the bag." It was my honor to serve with hundreds of professional non-commissioned officers who always made the officer corps look good. I truly believe they have the most critical job in the military.

Bonnie Joyce, our longtime executive assistant at The Brooks Group was instrumental in assisting Bill Brooks throughout the years and in working with the publisher.

Bethany DiLoreto, our Graphic Designer at The Brooks Group, enthusiastically applied her brilliant, creative and artistic skills to lay out the design of this book.

And of course, no acknowledgement would be complete without recognizing the support and contributions of my family. My wife, Jean, herself an Air Force officer and nurse, has encouraged me at every stage of my military and civilian careers. And my children, Philip and LeeAnne, who put up with my long hours, temporary duty assignments and several moves, and yet still look forward to their own military careers, have been a constant source of joy and pride.

About the Authors

Bill Brooks (1945 – 2007) was universally regarded as one of the most authoritative and respected sales writers in the world. A former award winning sales professional himself, he was the founder and CEO of The Brooks Group, a full service sales training and sales management education firm based in Greensboro, NC. Always in great demand as a speaker, Bill was a member of the Speaker Hall of Fame and a Certified Management Consultant. Mr. Brooks authored 19 other books on sales, sales management and related peak performance topics.

Kevin L. Reinert, Colonel, United States Air Force (Retired) is the Vice President for Government and Military Programs at The Brooks Group. He joined the organization in 2005, following a distinguished 28-year military career. Colonel Reinert was the Air Force Reserve Command Director of Public Affairs immediately prior to his military retirement. As senior spokesperson for a command with more than 70,000 personnel, Kevin was responsible for the Air Force Reserve's media relations, internal information, and community relations programs. Colonel Reinert earned his expertise on military recruiting first-hand. For more than 14 years, he was a highly-successful recruiting officer in both the active and reserve components, working enlisted, line officer and medical corps recruiting programs. His last recruiting assignment was serving as the vice commander of Air Force Reserve Command Recruiting Service at Robins Air Force Base, Georgia. It was there that he met Bill Brooks, and together in 2000 they introduced the Air Force Reserve recruiters to the IMPACT Selling® System. At the time, the Air Force Reserve had not made its annual recruiting goals in four consecutive years. Starting in Fiscal Year 2001, and every year since, the Air Force Reserve has exceeded its recruiting targets. In 2007, Kevin introduced the IMPACT Selling System to the Air National Guard, and in Fiscal Year 2008, the Air National Guard reached its end-strength target for the first time in five years. In 2009 Kevin was one of nine finalists for the American Business Awards' Sales Trainer of the Year.

Kevin can be reached at 800-633-7762, via e-mail at Kevin@thebrooksgroup.com or on the web at www.thebrooksgroup.com.

Chapter 1
Contemporary Military Recruiting

Welcome to the World of Military Recruiting

The introduction of the All-Volunteer Force in 1973 dramatically changed the methods by which America's armed forces filled their ranks. The shelving of the unpopular practice of conscription meant each branch would have to "*sell*" the merits of its recruiting opportunities to young Americans who now possessed the choice of whether or not to serve in the military. The first few years of the All-Volunteer Force were a struggle for the Department of Defense. Each of the branches often failed to meet numerical and quality goals. In an effort to market the value of military service, most armed forces advertising was done jointly, touting the military as the place to get "*experience*." Eventually, each of the services preferred to go their own way, using their marketing budgets to uniquely brand themselves and attract new recruits.

Although the failed policies of the Vietnam War tarnished the military's image in the 1960's and 70's, Americans eventually regained their admiration and respect for the men and women of the armed services after President Ronald Reagan took office in 1981. Higher salaries, united with quality of life initiatives, helped recruiting become somewhat easier for all the branches. However, now with America engaged in wars on two fronts, many young people, and their parents, are taking a closer look at the potential 'costs' of military service. One of the other great influences on the recruiting environment, in periods of war or peace, is the state of the economy. Booming economies make recruiting more difficult, while recessions have been known to create long lines of prospective applicants.

Perhaps the only constant recruiters can count on will be change, and we suspect the changes that will take place in the next decade will often occur with great speed and magnitude. Moreover, regardless of the political, social or economic conditions that will impact the recruiting marketplace, it will be up to the thousands of military recruiters across the nation to meet the procurement goals of the services they represent.

So, congratulations! If you're already a military recruiter, or in line to become one, your future is ripe with challenges. However, no matter what your level of recruiting experience, this book will introduce you to many valuable strategies and tactics.

What is Military Recruiting All About?

We said it before, but we'll say it again, military recruiting is selling. As a recruiter, you are a salesperson for your branch of service. You have many great tangible and intangible benefits to offer as part of the recruiting opportunity. However, those benefits come with a price, and in the case of the military, price is measured in terms of commitment. Applicants must serve a certain number of years, and during that time they give up certain personal freedoms and accept the obvious risks inherent to military service. Your task is to create enough value for the benefits of joining the military so that the benefits outweigh the price you're asking your applicants to pay. How do you do that? You do it by applying a sales system that calls for you to get in front of the right people with the right message at the right time. It's also properly positioning yourself and your organization. It's prospecting for leads, properly planning presentations and building trust with a wide range of qualified prospects and influencers. Additionally, your sales model must help you uncover the specific solutions your applicants are looking for while creating compelling value for the recruiting opportunities your service has to offer and the career fields that must be filled. It's also servicing your applicants in ways that exceed their expectations and leveraging them as referral sources. Those things don't happen by accident; you need a selling system to guide you every step of the way.

The Challenges Facing Military Recruiters

If anyone ever tells you a recruiter's job is easy, don't believe them. Today's recruiting environment is full of challenges. Whether you remain a recruiter for one tour of duty or for most of your career, you'll face a host of difficult issues. Here are just a few you may have to deal with:

- A growing intensity of competition for a smaller group of potential applicants
- Benefit-driven competition from other military branches and civilian opportunities
- Differentiating your branch of service from your competition
- Applicants who demand a 'hassle-free' recruiting experience
- Ever-changing economic, political and social conditions
- Prospects reluctant to make new or long commitments
- Limited job placement opportunities
- Prospects already armed with loads of information, thanks to the Internet
- Communicating the value of your recruiting opportunities to applicants who have other career choices
- Parents, spouses and other influencers who will play key roles in your applicant's decision-making process

The 20 Biggest Errors in Military Recruiting

Military recruiting may require a slightly different approach, based on which service you represent, the programs you're recruiting for (medical, enlisted, officer, active or reserve component, etc…), or the geographic location of the target market you're trying to penetrate.

Two Ways to Win
By far, the biggest mistakes recruiters make, no matter which service they work for, are either failing to invest enough time prospecting for new applicants or failing to ask enough of the right questions when they do get in front of qualified prospects.

However, regardless of the service or program you're recruiting for, here are 20 errors to avoid that could diminish your efforts:

1. Poor time management skills
2. Non-existent or inconsistent prospecting efforts
3. Too little pre-call planning before the recruiting interview
4. Failing to build adequate levels of trust and rapport with prospects
5. Inability to build productive relationships with the right influencers
6. Talking too much and listening too little, or not at all
7. Not asking enough of the right questions
8. Improperly applied or lack of product knowledge
9. Not knowing how to overcome objections
10. Recruiting without maintaining a focus on the applicant's wants and needs
11. Counting on your service's reputation as the main reason for selling or not selling the opportunity

12. Relying on incentives, instead of value, and overloading applicants with features and benefits that are irrelevant to their personal situations

13. Quoting the length of commitment before building value for the recruiting opportunity

14. High-pressure recruiting

15. Memorizing and applying 'canned' closing techniques

16. Making claims that can't be backed up by facts

17. Not revealing all the facts

18. Under-delivering on promises

19. Failing to ask your applicants to commit

20. Lack of continuation training

Put Yourself in a Position to Win
Knowing what <u>not</u> to do can be as valuable as knowing exactly what you should do. Smart recruiters work just as hard to keep from losing a fully qualified applicant as they do to find fully qualified applicants. Don't be your own worst enemy. Know the biggest errors – and avoid them.

The Seven Universal Rules for Military Recruiting Success

Now that we've listed the 20 biggest mistakes, you can avoid making them by following the seven universal rules stated below. They will serve you well, no matter your branch of service or target market you're recruiting into, as they have proven themselves successful with military recruiters all over the United States.

1. Proper positioning, prospecting and pre-call planning will place you in front of the right people, with the right message, at the right time.

2. Building trust with a prospect is rooted on the proper approach and not dominating the conversation.

3. Successful recruiting is based on asking enough of the right questions, in the right way, and not determining or presenting any solution until you have discovered:
   - What your prospects will commit to
   - How they'll commit
   - Why they'll commit, and
   - Under what conditions they'll commit

4. Properly presenting your solutions based on the conditions, terms and parameters under which your applicant will commit is the essence of a successful accession.

5. People expect recruiters to make claims for their branch of service. They are impressed, however, when someone else does, or when they experience those claims for themselves.

6. No accession is ever gained unless you ask your applicant to commit to joining.
7. There's still work to be done even after the applicant says "*Yes*" to the commitment.

How Loaded is Your Arsenal?
The recruiter's best weapons are their professional appearance, the energy to prospect, the interest to research prospects and the patience to learn about each prospect before the face-to-face interview ever starts.

The Universal Rules in Detail

Let's take a closer look at each of these rules.

Rule 1: Proper positioning, prospecting and pre-call planning will place you in front of the right people, with the right message, at the right time.

Top recruiters invest a lot of time in everything that occurs prior to getting face-to-face with a prospect. Marginally-performing recruiters tend to wait for prospects to find them and are subsequently ill-prepared to deal with their prospects in a knowledgeable way. For example, the best recruiters understand the power of networking, the Internet, referrals, and proactive school visitation programs as ways to prospect for business. They also grasp the differences between 'pull' and 'push' prospecting, and they realize that pull prospecting positions them better.

Positioning: The ranking or perception prospects have of you, your service's features and benefits or your branch of service, relative to your competition, both military and civilian.

Prospecting: The proactive steps taken to identify, isolate and get in front of qualified prospects.

Pre-Call Planning: The research, data-gathering and preparation you must complete to be prepared for a recruiting presentation.

Pull Prospecting: Attracting prospects through a broad-based process that could include such methods as public speaking, actively networking in community organizations and gaining celebrity status as a recruiting expert.

Push Prospecting: Contacting prospects one at a time, proactively, through such methods as direct mail, email or phone solicitation.

In the final analysis, people want to do business with you if you are a busy, highly-sought after professional far more

Knowledge Sells
It's far better to position yourself as a career counselor, military expert, advocate or creative problem solver than to position yourself simply as a military recruiter. Unfortunately, military recruiters are not positioned nearly as well in the marketplace as other professionals such as doctors and lawyers.

than if you appear to be a desperate, hungry, overly aggressive recruiter seeking to meet your 'quota' or 'goal.'

Pre-call planning is one of the most overlooked, yet fundamentally important, recruiting skills you can master. You need to gather essential information before you ever attempt to get in front of anyone, anywhere. Pull prospecting allows you the opportunity to invest more time in this process, because you can concentrate on the most valuable prospects – those who respond to you. If you are simply running up and down the street asking people to join, or waiting for the right person to appear on your doorstep, you have no time to invest into learning about someone and their background before you get face-to-face.

Vital Questions
Ideally, you should research the following issues before every interview:

* Is the person I'm meeting with capable of making their own decision or is there an influencer I should know about?
* Is the influencer a parent, spouse, boyfriend or girlfriend, employer, etc.?
* How much will the influencer be involved in the decision-making process?
* Who or what will I be competing against? Is it another branch of service, a civilian opportunity or a person close to the prospect?
* What questions is he or she likely to ask me?
* How can I develop internal advocacy through a parent, spouse, friend, etc.?
* What might the prospect find appealing about my branch of service?
* What might the prospect find unappealing?
* What is the biggest problem I can help the prospect solve?
* How far along is the prospect in the decision-making process?

Rule 2: Building trust with the prospect is rooted on the proper approach and not dominating the conversation.

In the military recruiting arena, building trust is far more important than just being liked. A fatal flaw for recruiters occurs when they believe they need to *"sell themselves to the prospect."* There's no need to tell an applicant how many awards you've won or how lucky the applicant is to be working with you. This is not correct; it's 'old school' recruiting and leads to the recruiter focusing on himself or herself, rather than the prospect. Think of it another way; once you're trusted, being liked generally follows anyway. Therefore, avoid trying to become just an approval-seeker.

Aim to Be Trusted
If you build trust, you're better positioned to sell value. Trust means the prospect has the belief, confidence, and full expectation that you (the recruiter) are a person of integrity and you and your organization will deliver everything you promise.

This doesn't, however, mean you should be rude, offensive or abrasive. And it also doesn't mean you need to be overly aggressive, dominate the conversation or be too friendly, too soon, either.

Rule 3: Military recruiting is based on asking enough of the right questions, in the right way, and not determining or presenting any solution until you have discovered:

- What your prospects will commit to
- How they'll commit
- Why they'll commit, and
- Under what conditions they'll commit

Don't Overwhelm
Good recruiters don't dominate the conversation or come across as too aggressive. Furthermore, they do not initiate 'unsolicited' small talk. If the prospect wants to talk, let him or her talk. If not, simply explain to the prospect why you requested the meeting and what you'd like to accomplish.

Outstanding recruiters excel at asking the right questions. They also concentrate on listening to their prospects' answers, recording their replies both in writing and mentally, and then prescribing the exact solutions their prospects are seeking, based on those responses. That is perhaps the most overlooked secret to successful recruiting.

Furthermore, one of the biggest errors you'll need to avoid is often referred to by veteran recruiters as 'benefits-dumping.' It's the tendency of a recruiter to prematurely start explaining all of the features and benefits their service offers, without knowing exactly what the prospect is interested in achieving or receiving. If you fall prey to this mistake, you'll lose far more accessions than you'll ever gain. You cannot presume you know exactly how to present your service's opportunities, unless you accurately know how your prospect wants to see them!

Understand First

Some recruiters make the mistake of providing solutions before learning about the prospect's unique situation, or worse, the person's qualifications to join in the first place. To guarantee you always ask your prospects enough of the right questions, in the right way, never conduct an interview or visit an influencer without prepared questions. And by no means should you attempt to ask for the commitment without knowing the answers to the four questions – What? How? Why? Under what conditions?

And the only way to do that is to ask the right questions.

Rule 4: Properly presenting your solution, based on the conditions, terms and parameters under which your prospect will commit, is the essence of a successful accession.

Smart recruiters understand there's a big difference between outdated demonstration recruiting where *"One size fits all"* and powerful, contemporary application-based recruiting. Once you internalize this truth, you're on your way to becoming a master recruiter.

Application-based Recruiting

Presenting your service's opportunities in the context of precisely how they can be applied to solve your prospect's biggest problem, agitation, difficulty or to address a solution they're seeking. It is far more than just focusing on features and benefits. Your prospects are looking for answers. Application-based recruiting is the essence of successful military recruiting.

People can only effectively focus on one thing at a time. And where you place that singular focus will greatly impact your recruiting success. Let's examine the four potential areas where you can focus:

1. Yourself: When you focus on yourself, you are likely more concerned with making your goal than satisfying your prospect's needs and wants.
2. The features and benefits: Rather than narrowing your focus on what's really important to the prospect, you simply recite the spectrum of features and benefits your service can offer, hoping the prospect will hear enough good things to make them want to commit.
3. Your branch of service: You should be proud of your branch of service and believe it to be the prospect's best option; however, until your prospect un-

derstands what makes your organization unique, all the services are the same to him or her. Besides, in an all-volunteer force, your prospects have choices, not only between branches, but also the choice not to join at all.

4. The prospect: By placing your focus on the prospect, you increase the likelihood of presenting the solutions your prospect is looking for. And when that happens, you dramatically increase the probability your prospect will commit.

The only way for you to take the correct actions is to commit 100% to building and sustaining a focus based solely on your prospects and applicants. You must be able to compartmentalize your life, and your thinking, so you can commit every phase of your presentation to the one point that drives recruiting success – a singular focus on your prospects – period.

Rule 5: People expect you to make claims for your branch of service. They are impressed, however, when someone

How Do You Focus?
Consider the following two scenarios. How do you focus appropriately?

First, you're having a bad morning and are in a miserable mood. Everything appears to be going wrong. Your child is sick, your car needs an expensive repair, and the bills are due. On this day, your focus is on yourself and how you must deal with these problems. However, you have an interview with a prospect at 1300 hours. How do you suddenly and easily shift gears?

Second, you just heard there's a possibility your recruiting office may be closed, and you might have to move to a different recruiting zone in another state. Where is your focus? Later today, you are speaking at a critical center-of-influence event with a group of high-level school officials, and you need to put on a great presentation. How do you shift your focus?

else does or if they experience your claims for themselves.
Recruiters have something to gain when someone agrees to join their branch of service. You know that and so do your prospects and applicants.

Unfortunately, lots of prospects and applicants have dealt with pushy salespeople or recruiters who stretched the truth or used high-pressure tactics, and they remember those experiences. These same people have become skeptical in any selling situation because they are tired of all the overselling they hear and see in the media.

Therefore, you must be in a position to offer your prospects and applicants the opportunity to talk to happy, satisfied people you've recruited, to read strong testimonials from them or to actually experience for themselves some of the benefits related to the opportunities and lifestyle your branch of service offers.

Developing Testimonials

To get satisfied people you've recruited to place their comments in writing, here's what you must do:

1. Convert prospects and applicants into accessions.
2. Service your prospects and applicants in ways that exceed their expectations.
3. Follow-up to be sure your accessions receive what you and your service have promised them.
4. Ask your accessions for strong references.
5. Thank your accessions and continue to keep in contact, if possible.

Select your testimonials with great care. Be sure they are strong and describe you, your recruiting opportunities and your branch of service in positive and powerful ways. That's why you must solicit these letters and comments only from highly-satisfied accessions.

Another method of maximizing testimonial support is asking your accessions to agree to be on a list of people you compile for prospects to contact, if they choose to do so. It's a very powerful way to involve your prospects with super-satisfied people who can verify your claims.

Tests and trials of your branch of service are especially valuable, since they allow people to experience your claims first-hand. However, when providing some sort of limited experience (e.g. base visit), be sure you

Get Your Accessions to Help You Recruit

To get the applicants you recruited to join the list of satisfied people prospects can contact, take the following steps:

- Solicit their involvement.
- Advise them you will rotate them off the list regularly.
- Ask them to provide their name, address, phone number or e-mail address.
- List the type of program or career field/occupational specialty you recruited them into.
- Promise to phone them in advance if you expect someone may contact them.
- Send them a thank you note whenever they talk with a prospect or applicant.

establish the parameters that define a successful trial and that you fully expect your applicants to commit, based on a successful outcome of the test.

Rule 6: No accession is ever gained unless you ask your applicant to join. In the final analysis, your success will be measured by how many people you enlist or commission. That means being assertive enough to ask someone to join your service branch.

How to Conduct Trials Without Errors

First clarify exactly what a successful outcome is. To do that, you need to:

1. Define what your prospect is looking for and what the test outcomes should be.
2. Establish a method for evaluating the results objectively.
3. Set the criteria the trial experience must meet for you to assume the applicant is pleased and ready to commit.

It's not unusual for recruiters to get caught up in the recruiting process and never ask the person to commit. In fact, research indicates approximately 65% of salespeople/recruiters can't bring themselves to ask for the sale or commitment. If you truly want to be successful, you must avoid that mistake at all costs. The real puzzle is to learn why so many recruiters go through the hard work of prospecting, getting in front of a qualified applicant, making a great presentation and then failing to ask the person to join. More often than not, it's the fear of rejection – don't be afraid to ask your applicant to commit!

Closing

Gaining your applicant's commitment is a consequence of what has happened earlier in the recruiting process. It's not a manipulative, climactic closing technique recruiters build toward. However, if you don't ask your applicants to commit, the majority will never make the decision on their own, because many people need help making important decisions. Consequently, you must urge your applicants to take action. Knowing this, you should suggest the steps your applicants need to take to come to a decision about joining.

Part of the foolishness of unprofessional recruiting is to teach someone the '20 Power Closes.' You are far better off mastering one statistically proven, non-manipulative tactic to finalize transactions rather than having a host of manipulative tricks you're hesitant to use, since they probably won't work anyway. Today's enlightened applicants can recognize when they're being manipulated, and when that happens, don't be surprised if they raise their defenses and ultimately decide not to commit.

Finally, remember this: if you don't ask your applicants to take action, nothing will happen! Instead, you will assume the role of professional host, visitor or tour guide. And you're none of those three. You're a professional military recruiter.

Rule 7: The real work begins after the applicant says "*Yes*."
The best recruiters know that servicing their applicants, exceeding expectations, anticipating problems and being available instantly are all part of the recruiting process, even though these events occur after the decision to commit is made. Hit-and-run recruiters don't

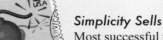

Simplicity Sells
Most successful recruiters use some form of the Assumptive Close. They don't use manipulating maneuvers. Old school recruiting suggested you learn the continuous agreement close, Ben Franklin close, impending event close, etc. Statistically, it's best to act as if the applicant has agreed to commit. Simply say or ask some form of the following:

*   Would you like to go ahead and get started?
*   Let me show you how we can move ahead.
*   Should we handle the paperwork now?

understand this at all. Their philosophy is to promise whatever is necessary to get the applicant to commit, gain the accession credit at any cost and then do all in their power to avoid dealing with that applicant again. The old "*Kiss 'em and ship 'em*" philosophy no longer works in today's recruiting environment. Applicants who feel they were mistreated will complain to military authorities, friends, family and anyone else who will listen, including media outlets and groups that oppose military recruiters. The word will get back to you, and your reputation will be severely damaged.

Earning accessions is hard work. Your mission is to convert prospects to applicants, then to accessions and to keep them happy throughout the process. In fact, you want your newest accessions so pleased they will cheerfully refer you to more prospects like them and agree to serve as testimonial sources to help your recruiting efforts.

However, to earn this right, you must establish long-term relationships based on superior service, total integrity, and commitment to delivering what you promised. Unfortunately, some recruiters don't seem to understand this universal rule or maybe they just don't believe it. It's really the difference between transactional recruiting and relationship recruiting. Never forget, your future recruiting efforts are dependent on how you handle every person you meet. A sound word of advice we offer every recruiter is to treat all their applicants as though it were their own son or daughter who was being recruited into military service.

One recommendation is to make regular follow-up calls to your applicants – not just the ones where your goal is to ensure your applicants are still in town, within weight standards or haven't done something that disqualifies them from reporting for duty. Regular contact is a good way to find out if your applicant, or their parents, or their spouse have any questions before they get upset and raise complaints. Moreover, you should also contact the family while your new accession is away at military training. You may learn something about how you handled this applicant that can help you in the future. It's even smart to send a personal note. Such simple steps help build relationships by going above and beyond what your applicants and their families would normally expect from the average military recruiter.

Military Recruiting as a Profession and Where You Fit In

Military Recruiting is a profession. It's more than just a job, career field, military occupational specialty or special duty assignment. And, as a profession, it provides the opportunity for significant personal satisfaction, a good income and exceptional prestige, if you are a top producer. The profession also requires specialized skills and training for superior performance, and it allows you to bring great value to many people.

Recruit with Integrity
To ensure you feel good about what you do and how you do it, the skills you learn and apply must be consistent with your value system and the core values of the service you represent. Applying manipulative techniques flies in the face of the way most people in today's society want to feel about themselves. It also creates a situation where you don't believe in what you do or you don't feel good about doing it. This is demotivating. Avoid it at all costs.

However, for you to get the most enjoyment from the military recruiting profession, you need to believe in what you do and how you do it. And you must believe the skills and strategies you master are credible, professional and honorable.

You can begin by employing an applicant-focused recruiting process based on sound and honorable principles that allows you to feel good about what you do and how you do it. It's the first step to becoming a top performer in one of our nation's most important professions.

Checklist for Chapter 1

☐ Military recruiting is selling, and it's all about getting in front of the right people, with the right message, at the right time.

☐ Today's recruiting environment is ripe with challenges you will have to overcome.

☐ Regardless of which service you represent or program you're recruiting into, you must avoid the 20 biggest errors.

☐ Following the seven universal rules will help you avoid the 20 biggest errors.

☐ Recruiting requires positioning yourself and your branch of service, prospecting for leads, properly planning your presentations, building trust, and uncovering the right set of answers your applicants are looking for. It's also making your answers or solutions available to them under the conditions and terms which they are most interested in committing. Next, it's offering proof that everything you have promised is true, followed by asking for the commitment and then servicing your new accessions in ways that exceed their expectations.

☐ Military recruiting is a profession, not just a job, career field, military occupational specialty or special duty assignment. Recruiting duty provides the opportunity for significant personal satisfaction, a good income and exceptional prestige, if you are a top producer. Recruiting duty also requires specialized skills and training for superior performance.

☐ Military recruiters must have integrity. Be sure everything you do or say is consistent with your value system and the core values of the service you represent.

Chapter 2
Military Recruiting: The Insider Secrets

How valuable would it be if you learned the most essential secret to becoming a successful military recruiter? What if you could master the one simple truth more than 95% of all salespeople in the world, including military recruiters, have no idea even exists, let alone have any clues about how to implement?

First, you would slice years off of your learning curve. Second, you would be equipped with a unique insight to instantly propel your recruiting career.

But shockingly, you would also be handed a huge burden. You're probably asking yourself, *"Burden? How could something so valuable prove to be a burden?"* The burden is the responsibility that such a powerful insight can place on you, because knowing a universal success secret and not implementing it would be equal to committing career suicide. Failing at anything when you know precisely how to be successful at it is unacceptable.

The good news is this insight, along with hundreds of professional secrets, will be revealed in great detail throughout the remaining chapters of this book. But, for now, let's settle for a quick look at this career-changing truth.

Recruiting's Biggest Success Secret Revealed

The secret to successful recruiting is to be in front of qualified prospects when they're ready to commit, not when you need to make your goal.

Are you surprised by that simple, yet profound principle? To help you better understand what's behind this truth, we'll break the statement into its three fundamental parts. You need to:

1. be in front of qualified prospects…
2. when they're ready to commit…
3. not when you need to make your goal!

Think back to one of your own major buying experiences. You probably decided to make that purchase when you thought you could afford it (qualified) and when you wanted that product or service (ready to commit). However, it's doubtful you were concerned about the salesperson's goal. Your task is to find prospects when

Don't Waste Your Time

Smart recruiters don't waste a lot of time in front of prospects who don't possess all of the qualifying characteristics. Suppose a person called you and said, "*I really like what your service has to offer. Could I come see you today?*" Would you be excited about already having gained an accession or would you ask the person a few questions like the following:

- "*What made you decide to look into the _____ (military branch)?*"
- "*What have you seen that's interesting or appealing to you?*"
- "*Where are you in the decision-making process?*"
- "*What factors will go into your decision to consider joining the _____ (military branch)?*"
- "*What kind of timeframe are you working with?*"
- "*Who else, other than you, is involved in this decision?*"

Just a few simple questions like those above will help you determine if this prospect is on the right track to becoming a fully-qualified applicant. For example, by getting the answers to these questions you'll find out if the prospect is aware of any needs, whether or not they have the authority to make the decision on their own, and if there's a relative sense of urgency.

Additionally, it's wise (and necessary) to ask preliminary qualifying questions, once you've developed some rapport with the prospect on the phone. If the prospect offers the 'right' (non-disqualifying) answers to the physical, mental, and moral qualifying questions, attempt to schedule a face-to-face appointment. Should the prospect agree to meet, you know they will listen to you, and hopefully you're on your way to establishing a significant level of trust. However, always remember that it's much easier to raise the trust level when you meet in person.

they are qualified and ready, not when you're an accession or two short of making your mission.

The Five Characteristics of Qualified Prospects

Have you ever tried to recruit someone who wasn't qualified to join? Being 'qualified' means your prospects exhibit five critical characteristics:
1. The have a need for what you offer and are aware of it.
2. They have both the authority to make the decision and ability to qualify for the opportunity.
3. They have a relative sense of urgency about the decision.
4. They trust you and your branch of service.
5. They are willing to listen to you.

Your best prospects will have all five of these characteristics at the same time. Those with fewer will become progressively less qualified as more of the characteristics disappear. For example, a prospect with four of the five is better than one with just three. Three is better than two, and two is better than one. The secret, though, is to invest most of your time with prospects that have all five.

The biggest challenge you'll face is to avoid settling for being in front of prospects who only possess characteristic #5 – they are simply willing to listen to you. Be careful not to fall prey to the temptation to pile up appointments simply for the sake of hollow opportunities. Unfortunately, some recruiters mistakenly believe that recruiting is just a 'numbers game.' It's not. It's also very much about quality, and successful recruiters understand that fact.

The Power of an Understood Need

You must be in front of prospects that have a need and are aware of it. Just ask any experienced recruiter how successful they have been at trying to 'create' a need, and you will learn how fruitless that effort can be. Working with prospects who tell you they need a job because they just lost theirs, and listening to prospects tell you they need educational benefits to earn a college degree, are much better scenarios.

The Beauty of Both the Authority and Ability to Qualify for the Opportunity

Have you ever tried to recruit someone with the authority to join but no ability to qualify? How about no authority and lots of ability? The results are the same – no accession. The only thing worse is to be in front of someone who has neither authority nor ability.

On the other hand, when you meet with someone who has both the authority to make the decision and the ability to qualify for the recruiting opportunity, you are in the right zone. That's where your efforts can really pay off. Nevertheless, don't assume prospects who meet the age of consent can make the decision to join on their own. Many applicants are going to ask their parents, spouse, relatives or close friends for advice. Be sure to ask who these people might be, and invite them to be part of the recruiting process.

The Urgency Factor

Urgency can have great value. It sometimes forces prospects into doing things they may have previously viewed as being difficult, overwhelming or demanding. There is, however, another truth about urgency: a recruiter can't force any false sense of urgency on a prospect. Today's applicants are too sophisticated for the old school recruiting ploy that said create a false sense of urgency with state-ments like, "*The enlistment bonus you're interested in could go away tomorrow, so if I were you, I'd commit to joining today,*" or "*I've got only one opening left in this career field* (when you really have three openings); *you'd better take it this minute because no one knows if you'll get another opportunity to get the job you want tomorrow.*" Urgency must be legitimate, self-identified and owned by the prospect.

Trust Versus Like

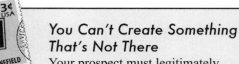

You Can't Create Something That's Not There

Is it more important for you to be liked or trusted? We hope you said trusted, because it's not even a close contest. Trust is essential. In fact, in today's competitive recruiting marketplace, it may be the most important factor. Being liked merely means your prospects may listen to what you have to say, but not necessarily believe enough in you or the service you represent to

Your prospect must legitimately feel a sense of urgency; you cannot artificially create it. That's manipulation. And manipulation isn't recruiting; it's deceitful and dishonest. For example: "*If you can't make up your mind today, you may never see another opportunity like this ever again.*" What type of reaction do you think this kind of artificial play would elicit in today's recruiting environment where every prospect has multiple branches of service to choose from, as well as potential opportunities outside of the military?

make a commitment. These same prospects are more likely to continue 'shop-ping' for the tangible benefits or what they see as the 'easiest' or 'shortest' com-mitment, the 'biggest bonus,' or the 'largest' educational assistance package.

One the other hand, being trusted means you can sell value, because your applicants believe in you, your service and the intangible, as well as tangible, opportunities you offer. They also trust you to point out why your opportunity is 'different' or 'better' than the competition, even though on the surface the competition appears to offer a better deal. Value is a far superior selling tool—100% of the time—you can bet on it.

It's All About Their Time Frame, Not Yours

Ask just about any recruiter how soon they'd like their applicants to be ready to commit, and a very high percentage will answer *"Right away."* Unfortunately, most applicants, if they do agree to commit, will do so when they want to, not necessarily when you want them to. While you're hoping the recruiting process is the most important thing going on in the lives of your applicants, they might have other ideas. Their focus could be on enjoying their summer vacation, a family member's upcoming

War of Wills: You Lose
When a prospect and recruiter engage in a war of wills, the recruiter will lose. For example, if you start dictating terms, conditions, requirements or limitations your prospects see as unreasonable, don't be surprised if they walk out the door. It's an all-volunteer force, and your prospects have choices. The law of supply and demand is on their side and working against you.

wedding, concerns expressed by their spouse or conditions they're experiencing at work.

Know the Processing Cycle
If you want to realize consistent success month after month, first analyze the length of your processing cycle. That's the average length of time it takes you to turn a qualified lead into an accession. For example, let's say your average processing time is 60 days from receiving a lead to getting that person to enlist. Now, pretend it's the beginning of February. At this point, you shouldn't be planning how you will make your February goal. You ought to be working on your April goal, because your data indicates that's when your current leads will be ready to join. Every month, based on your goals, you must schedule your activities to achieve the results you need two months into the future. Do this analysis every month, and you will experience consistent recruiting months sequentially down the road. On the other hand, if you fail to analyze your processing times and how they impact your recruiting activities, you will never get any traction in the future.

Now some recruiters might argue that you should encourage your applicants to brush those personal issues aside and then push them into making a decision – bad idea. Pushy recruiters will lose far more accessions than they ever make.

It's Not About When You Need to Make Your Goal

One of the most curious dynamics of recruiting is the role that panic plays in a recruiter's performance. Yes. Pure, outright panic!

Based on your how your goaling schedule is designed, you may sometimes find yourself with too few days left in the month or quarter and not enough applicants in the pipeline. What's the result? You're not going to make your mission. You need to gain some accessions—and fast.

Unfortunately, prospects don't care about your recruiting goals. And truthfully, you created this problem yourself. You're the one who failed to be in front of enough qualified prospects when they were ready to commit. So don't point the finger at others; look in the mirror.

The Two Most Essential Components of Military Recruiting

The two most essential components for getting your prospects to commit are 'positioning' and 'timing.' It's ironic that these two components are factors you may not even associate with recruiting. As a result, they are far too often overlooked and vastly undervalued. But once you understand and master them, everything else in recruiting becomes easier.

Who's In Control?
Never forget, people join the military for their reasons and according to their time schedules. They don't join for your reasons or when you need to make your recruiting goal. Your task is to find out what recruiting opportunity they want, when they want to join, why they will join, under what conditions they will join and then provide it to them on those terms and within their time frame. The key is to get all of this information from the prospect and then package your solution in those terms. Your challenge is to ask the right questions to get the answers on how to present your solution. It's really that simple; don't make it any more difficult.

Positioning

This is an important strategic advantage too few recruiters understand or apply. One of life's fundamental truths is that perception is reality. Therefore, you should invest lots of time and energy to create an image of yourself that keeps prospects from perceiving you as just a military recruiter. Ask 100 people on the street to respond to their perception of the words 'military recruiter,' and there's a pretty good chance their responses won't all be flattering.

Your personal positioning is one advantage you could easily overlook, but it could be the most valuable instrument in your toolkit. Smart recruiters know the value of personal positioning and use it as a strategic advantage.

The essential components of positioning include such things as the appearance of your uniform, your military bearing and image, manners, timeliness, responsiveness, expertise, knowledge and problem-solving abilities.

JARGON

What is Positioning All About?

As mentioned in Chapter 1, positioning is the relative ranking or perception that prospects, applicants and influencers have of you, your opportunities, and/or your branch of service relative to your competition. With that said, there's personal positioning and service positioning. Personal positioning is how people view you compared to other recruiters they've met. Service positioning is how people think about the military branch you represent. On the personal positioning side, are you considered equal to, better than, inferior to, or somewhat like other military recruiters you compete against? On the service side, are you seen as representing a 'high-tech' service or a 'warrior' service? Either way is fine. However, you must be aware of what the public thinks of you and your service branch so you can decide how to approach your target markets.

THREAT REDUCTION

Add Value

People pay attention to individuals whom they perceive as having something important to say to them. Consequently, it's to your advantage to be perceived as someone who brings value to any relationship. Great recruiters position themselves as something other than just recruiters. They posture themselves as career counselors, trusted advisors, advocates, military experts and creative problem solvers. In those additional roles, they are seen as important people who contribute valuable expertise. Prospects will often seek them out to gain access to their knowledge and their recruiting opportunities just happen to go along with it.

They are all assets you need to pay very careful attention to on a regular basis. Here are some more: How neat and clean is your government vehicle? Do you have to apologize for its condition every time you transport an applicant? Are your recruiting tools organized and spotless, or are they stained, dog-eared and/or out-of-date?

The personal positioning concept incorporates everything related to the views others have of you—in macro (e.g. expert or advisor), micro (Are you always on time or are you late?) and mini ways (Are your nails clean?). Overlook these things and your prospect will overlook you.

Timing

We've already mentioned timing; however it's so important, it bears repeating. Like positioning, timing is often undervalued. But what does it mean?

In competitive recruiting markets and turbulent economic, political and social times, it's not unusual for someone to quickly and unexpectedly need the opportunities the military has to offer. People lose jobs, encounter changes in family

Sergeant Hilton vs. Sergeant Smith
Sergeants Hilton and Smith both recruit for different services in the same city.

Hilton believes cold-calling school lists and ASVAB rosters are good ways to find new applicants, and it's been her primary prospecting strategy for five years. She literally works the phone all day long and into the evening, sometimes making 50 to 60 calls a day. Hilton occasionally pays a visit to her assigned schools where she gets those lists, just to keep a personal touch with the people who provide her with those names.

Meanwhile, Smith is active in several community service organizations, including the American Legion, the Red Cross as a volunteer and the Chamber of Commerce. Smith has even been the guest speaker during public ceremonies honoring military veterans on various Federal holidays. And since she was a combat medic prior to becoming a recruiter, Smith also teaches first-aid classes at her church and the YMCA. She has been in the marketplace competing with Hilton for only two years.

Which recruiter do you think is positioned better in the community, Sergeant Hilton or Sergeant Smith? Which recruiter do you think people would be more likely to visit or advise their friends or children to see?

Top-of-Consciousness
When your prospects consider joining the military, how do you and your branch of service stack up? Do they think of you first, last or never? By achieving top-of-consciousness, you become the recruiter they think of most often, and that's the status you should be aiming for.

status or perhaps identify a need for experience and education they can't get or afford anywhere else. When events like these happen and cause people to recognize an unfilled need, you want to be the first person they think of who can help them. This is where your personal positioning becomes valuable.

Proper positioning includes building and sustaining strategies that make people aware of who you are and what you can offer them. When you achieve 'top-of-consciousness' status with your prospects, you become the marketplace's recruiter of choice when they are ready to commit.

Nevertheless, we recognize you can't be everywhere at once. So, what can you do? Answer: Build 'recruiting surrogates' who are in front of your prospects when you aren't. Employ digital tools like email, cell-phones, voice mail, text messaging and Internet websites that put you and/or your branch of service in

Getting Out In Front
Tactics that place you in front of prospects and influencers as often and as smoothly as possible are essential, because you often won't know when people may suddenly and urgently need your recruiting opportunity.

Here are some tools you can use:

- Your own digital newsletter with informative articles on subjects your prospects and influencers are likely interested in
- Holiday cards, birthday cards, graduation cards (mailed or digital)
- Your organization's Website. Be sure your contact information is correct.
- E-mail or text message updates
- Professional and social networking Websites (Be cautious about the personal information and/or photos you upload.)

The key is that your process must be consistent and persistent—but you must never be a pest. For example, never spam! Instead, make sure whatever information you deploy is helpful, meaningful and positive. Remember that you're fighting for mind share, but always fight fair and square!

front of prospects when you're not available. You can't always be where they are, but you can stay on their mind.

The Importance of a Consistent Sales Approach

Recruiting is one of the most important duty assignments you can be assigned to, and because the job is so vital, you will receive additional money each month for your efforts. The extra income is just one incentive you have to be successful. In some branches, top performers can remain as recruiters for as long as they continue to meet mission requirements.

What do you think successful 'career' recruiters have in common? How about a consistent sales process? On the other hand, failing recruiters generally do not practice a consistent sales process. What would you think of a surgeon who told you before an operation, "*I don't have a process or system for this surgery—I just improvise*"? You would probably have big doubts about the success of the surgery, and you would probably find another surgeon, really fast!

In your own recruiting career perhaps you might have this experience: you say or do something a certain way in the morning and successfully gain a commitment. Then you do the same thing in the afternoon, but it doesn't work. Was there a big difference between the prospect who said "*Yes*" in the morning and the one who said "*No*" in the afternoon? Of course not. The problem is you probably 'improvised' in the morning, stumbled on something that worked in that situation, and then 'improvised' again in the afternoon with the same grab-bag approach. But because it wasn't tested, proven and carefully developed, it wasn't ready for prime time, and it failed with the second applicant. Now you're back to square one again looking for another approach.

Don't Use Scripts

Don't use a scripted, memorized recruiting presentation or a never-ending, static, digital slide show. These are nothing but electronic flipcharts. Inflexible presentations lock you into an approach that doesn't let you adjust your interaction with the prospect. Instead, you need an elastic process that allows you to modify your presentation as you learn more about your prospect. We're talking about a sequential system that consistently follows the same format or process but allows you the flexibility to be sure your presentation is 100% on target to address your prospect's priorities, needs, problems or most important solutions.

If you don't know exactly where you're going, you'll probably wind up somewhere other than where you want to be. That's also true if you know where you want to end up but don't have a roadmap that tells you how to get there. The truth is you need to have a carefully-prescribed strategy for both prospecting and selling.

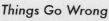

Things Go Wrong

Sergeant Johnson was convinced his presentation to the high school seniors was perfect. He had prepared it a week ahead of time. It was very close to being his standard presentation, and he knew it cold – 42 slides, all carefully loaded onto a laptop computer. He double-checked his equipment before the presentation to be sure it worked and was satisfied he was ready.

However, two minutes before going on stage, he encountered a few unforeseen problems. And they weren't technical! The school principal was apologetic, but he advised Johnson he now had only 20 minutes to speak, not the 50 he was promised last week. It seems the previous speaker went over his time limit. And, instead of discussing the 'college education financial assistance' features Johnson had built his entire presentation around, the principal asked him to talk about gender diversity and equal opportunity in the military. Unfortunately, Sergeant Johnson had only one presentation in his toolkit. What could he do?

The Six Principles That Can Guide Your Recruiting Career

These six principles, when applied consistently and regularly, will virtually guarantee your long-term professional success. Furthermore, these principles aren't gimmicks or tricks that only work once in a while or are so manipulative as to render them marginally ethical.

Outdated Techniques: Don't Use!

- If I could show you a way to pay for college you'd be interested, wouldn't you?"
- "The sale begins when the prospect says 'No'."
- "An objection is the sign of a closed mind and a consequence of something that has happened far earlier in the sale."
- "Learn the ABC's of recruiting... <u>A</u>lways <u>B</u>e <u>C</u>losing!"
- "Memorize 12 ways to close and 15 ways to overcome objections, and you will recruit well."
- "Sell yourself first. All else will follow."
- "The one who speaks first loses."

Principle #1: You Must Align Your Prospecting and Selling Strategies

Top recruiters think strategically. So first remember that successful recruiting stems from the number of qualified prospects you get in front of and how effective you are when you are in front of them. Here are two essential definitions top-performing recruiters master:

- Prospecting is the strategy and systems you use to get in front of qualified prospects.
- Selling is what you do when you are in front of qualified prospects.

Honest, Contemporary Principles: Use!

- "People join the military for their reasons, not yours."
- "Gaining the commitment is the result of effective positioning, prospecting, pre-call planning, building trust, asking the right questions, selling value and sustaining credibility."
- "In the absence of the perception of value, every negotiation will degenerate to the issue of price. In a military recruiting environment, price is measured in terms of the commitment the prospect must make to join the service."
- "Begin with trust and all else will follow."

To make these two work hand-in-hand, it's essential to understand and apply them as shown in Figure 2-1:

Selling Strategy

	Inconsistent	Consistent
Prospecting Strategy — Consistent	Failure	Limited Opportunities
Prospecting Strategy — Inconsistent	Minimal Yield	High Performance Results

Figure 2-1: Effective Prospecting and Selling Strategic Matrix

The prospecting strategy, on the left axis, can be either inconsistent or consistent. Inconsistent means you don't regularly apply the same, proven strategies that usually yield prospects who exhibit the five common characteristics of qualified prospects. When this occurs, you won't have a steady flow of people to get in front of and give your sales presentation. Meanwhile, a consistent prospecting strategy has a greater chance of yielding a greater number of highly qualified prospects.

Your selling strategy, along the top axis, works in a similar fashion. An inconsistent sales process will yield the poor results. You'll sell successfully in some instances and falter badly at other times. However, when you apply a highly-effective selling strategy on a regular basis, your success rates will improve.

Because prospecting and selling are so mutually dependent, you cannot separate the two. As for the results, the diagram clearly shows you. Where do you think you need to be?

Equations for Failure and Success

Inconsistent Prospecting Effort + Inconsistent Sales Effort = Failure

Consistent Prospecting Effort + Inconsistent Sales Effort = Minimal Yield

Inconsistent Prospecting + Consistent Sales Effort = Limited Recruiting Opportunities

Consistent Prospecting Effort + Consistent Sales Effort = High Performance Results

Principle #2: People Don't Always Buy What They Need; They Always Buy What They Want

Think about this for a minute. Do most people eat fresh fruits (what they need) or candy bars (what they want)? Do they eat bran muffins (what they need) or sugar-coated doughnuts (what they want)? Do they prefer to buy beer or milk? Do they initially work to solve problems they really need to solve or the ones they want to solve?

Don't be falsely-consumed trying to address only your prospects' needs. Pure needs-based selling is a myth. If prospects only bought what they needed, there would be little room left for the emotional side of selling. Needs are rational, while wants are extremely emotional—and sales are really all about emotions, aren't they?

Here are some examples: You need a car. You prefer to buy the one you want. You need a suit. You buy the one you want. You need a vacation. You go to the destination where you want to go.

Knock It Off!
Don't begin a recruiting presentation with the phrase, "*I'm here to meet your needs.*" Instead, see what happens when you tell your prospect, "*My job is to help you get what you want.*" You'll be amazed by the attentive response you'll get. You'll learn more about why this is important in the next chapter.

Principle #3: Don't Begin Your Sales Presentation with Unsolicited Small Talk.

Our in-depth research proves beyond the shadow of any doubt that most prospects are put off by 'unsolicited' small talk. What's the key here? If your prospect wants to engage in small talk, let him or her do so. However, don't you be the one who offers it!

Have you ever seen how awkward it is to move from 'small talk' to 'sales talk'? It's like switching gears in a cheap car—awkward, noisy, grinding and obvious.

Avoid looking for something in your prospect's immediate environment to talk about. Don't try to find 'common ground.' The truth is that every other recruiter who has ever been with that prospect has asked about their favorite sports team, the traffic or remarked about the weather. And every one has been labeled as a 'me too' recruiter. You need to avoid that label altogether and become a category of one.

So, what should you say? It's simple. Just tell your prospect what you'd like to accomplish during the appointment. After all, that's really the common ground that brought you together in the first place, isn't it?

Here are three examples:

- "*I'd like to have a chance to get to meet you, ask you a few questions, answer any questions you might have and see if there is some way we may be able to help you.*"
- "*I'd like to meet you today, ask you a few questions, answer your questions and find out if becoming a member of the (branch of service) is something you might be interested in.*"
- "*I'd like a chance to ask you a few questions, determine if we can help you and find out if becoming a member of the (branch of service) is a viable option for you.*"

Principle #4: Most Selling Occurs Early in the Sales Process.

Sales are made or lost much earlier in the conversation than most people think. That may surprise you. It may also astound you to learn most selling occurs at times when it looks like no selling is occurring at all. The first time is during the pre-call planning phase, where the depth of information you acquire

GOOD PLANNING

Everything Starts with the Three P's
Never overlook the important functions of prospecting, positioning and pre-call planning, whether you are meeting a new prospect or an existing applicant. That's because in the competitive world of recruiting, the recruiter who has the most information and knows how to use it usually wins the accession. Information obtained in the early stages of the selling process also prepares you to ask the right questions during your face-to-face interview, thus allowing you to discover what your prospect or applicant wants to have happen.

prepares you for an effective appointment. The second time is when you begin to ask critical questions that allow your prospect to identify and verbalize what, how, when and why they'll commit to the recruiting opportunity.

In the face-to-face side of recruiting, the critical information you gather before the interview becomes very useful as you start asking questions that allow your prospects to tell you what they'll commit to, when they'll commit, how they'll commit and under what conditions they'll commit.

DANGER MINES

MINEFIELD

Don't Stop Short
The tendency to stop asking questions before obtaining enough information to prescribe the exact solutions your prospect is looking for could prevent you from gaining the commitment. In fact, it's the biggest reason why recruiters fail when they are face-to-face with prospects. Unskilled recruiters will ask one or two questions, assume they know their prospect's problems or needs, and then shoehorn a solution of their own design. A top recruiter, on the other hand, draws out the prospect's innermost needs, wants, problems and desires through meaningful questions and then prescribes a targeted solution that addresses all their concerns. That's the difference between winning and losing the accession.

It may sound strange to talk about the three P's (prospecting, positioning and pre-call planning) when you're dealing with existing applicants – people you've already tested, physicaled and perhaps even sworn into a delayed enlistment or delayed entry program. However, it's not strange, it's required! You must constantly be battling for mindshare, knowledge and an advantage with both new prospects and existing applicants. Don't ever forget that your best prospects and applicants are also someone else's top prospects! And more than a few applicants have been known to change their minds at the last minute.

Some old school recruiters will tell you the key to gaining commitment is how well you 'dazzle 'em' with your presentation and how adept you are at using multiple ways to close the sale. We have lots of research from the public and private sector that shows exactly the opposite. Thousands of prospects, customers and applicants were asked what they would like to have seen their salesperson or recruiter do differently. The overwhelming response was *"Open the sale better."* Further-

Mindshare
How much of your prospect's or applicant's conscious or unconscious thought is directed toward you and the recruiting opportunity you're offering?

Your goal is to own as much mindshare as possible. Closely related to the top-of-consciousness principle, mindshare will dictate how much attention you will receive from a person.

more, among the very top sales and recruiting professionals we observed, the vast majority use one simple closing technique – not 12. We'll have lots more to say about opening and closing the sale later in this book.

Planning Is Key
Truth be known, the sale is generally won or lost before you get in front of a prospect. Also, never forget the initial part of the face-to-face interview is far more important than rushing to close the sale.

Principle #5: The Most Essential Face-To-Face Recruiting Skills You Can Ever Master are the Skills to Ask Questions, Listen to the Answers and Never Interrupt!

Let's be very clear: recruiting is far more about asking and listening than telling and talking. But here's the problem: too many recruiters don't get it. They believe it's all about being talkative, persuasive, and verbally aggressive. But it's not.

And to make matters worse, lots of recruiters (perhaps even you) have been told silly things like *"You've got the gift of gab; you ought to go into recruiting"* or *"With that silver tongue, you ought to be a recruiter."* Very few people are ever told, *"You have the gift of asking the right questions, shutting up, listening to the answers and then asking more questions! You should become a recruiter."*

This is a case where conventional knowledge is all wrong. It's counterintuitive; what seems like it should work doesn't work, and what you might not expect to work will take you to great success.

Principle #6: You Must Have a Linked, Sequential Process that You Follow in Every Recruiting Interview, Every Time, Without Fail

Keep It Simple
Never interrupt a prospect. On the other hand, you must always be interruptible. Ask the right questions. Ask permission to write down the answers. Use more questions to determine the exact 'buying' parameters of your prospect. Then, you simply repeat back the key points they told you. Never forget, they will join your branch of service for their reasons, not yours. Recruiting is really that simple.

Regrettably, far too many recruiters don't have the patience to follow a sequential selling process. Also, many sales models taught today are too complex or confusing. For example, have you ever been taught that there are 12 steps to the sale? Simple and shorter are better. And it's also true that sometimes less is more.

Since 1977, we have successfully taught an easy-to-follow process that more than 500,000 salespeople and recruiters around the world have used to advance their careers. Since 2000, we have successfully taught a customized version of that same process to more than 1,500 military recruiting and retention personnel from the Air Force Reserve (introduced in 2000) and the Air National Guard (introduced in 2007). The process has been taught to people who sell both tangible products and intangible services, people who sell both big ticket and less expensive products and people who engage in both simple and complex sales. It makes no difference.

You, too, need a process that allows you to move through the sale easily and quickly, a process that's empowers you to be in control and allows you to know where you are going next in the recruiting process. Without a system, your presentations will be inconsistent (remember that!) and so will your results.

The process we teach is called the IMPACT Selling System®. (William T. Brooks, High Impact Selling: Power Strategies for Successful Selling, GamePlan Press, 1988) It is broken down as follows:

- **I**nvestigate – prospecting, positioning, pre-call planning
- **M**eet – engaging the prospect, establishing rapport and building trust

- **Probe** – asking the right questions so you can recommend a solution and gain commitment
- **Apply** – recommending a solution that addresses your prospect's greatest need or want
- **Convince** – maximizing social proof and allowing your prospect to experience the truth of your claims through third-party corroboration
- **Tie-It-Up** – asking for the commitment, finalizing the transaction, cementing and reinforcing the decision to commit

The IMPACT System has three simple rules:

- Don't skip a step.
- Make sure you and your prospect are in the same step at the same time.
- Don't leave a step until you have completed that step.

A simple and consistent sales process will work if you diligently apply it. We'll show you, in great detail, exactly how to implement this sales model and make your recruiting career fun, satisfying and successful. However, all of this valuable information will stay between the covers of this book if you don't learn and apply it. That choice is up to you.

Checklist for Chapter 2

☐ The secret to successful recruiting is to be in front of qualified prospects when they're ready to commit, not when you need to make your goal.
☐ Qualified prospects exhibit five critical characteristics:
  1. They have a need for what you offer and are aware of it.
  2. The have both the authority and ability to qualify for the opportunity.
  3. The have a relative sense of urgency about the decision.
  4. They trust you and your branch of service.
  5. They are willing to listen to you.
☐ Smart recruiters don't waste a lot of time in front of prospects who don't possess all of the five characteristics.
☐ Being liked merely means your prospects may listen to what you have to say, but not necessarily believe enough in you or the service you represent to make a commitment. Being trusted means you can sell true value, because your applicant believes in you, your service and the intangible, as well as tangible, opportunities you offer.
☐ People join the military for their reasons, not yours, and according to their time schedules.

☐ The two most essential components for getting your prospects to commit are positioning and timing.

☐ Six principles that can guide your recruiting career:
1. You must align your prospecting and selling strategies.
2. People don't always buy what they need; they always buy what they want.
3. Don't begin your sales presentation with unsolicited small talk.
4. Most selling occurs early in the sales process.
5. The most essential face-to-face recruiting skills you can ever master are to ask questions, listen to the answers and never interrupt!
6. You must have a linked, sequential process that you follow in every recruiting interview, every time, without fail.

☐ The IMPACT Selling System consists of six steps:
1. **Investigate**
2. **Meet**
3. **Probe**
4. **Apply**
5. **Convince**
6. **Tie-It-Up**

☐ The IMPACT System has three rules:
1. Don't skip a step to get to any other step.
2. Make sure you and your prospect (applicant) are in the same step at the same time.
3. Don't leave a step until you have completed that step.

Chapter 3
Focus, Alignment and Leverage

"I'm here to meet your needs." It's as old as the hills and one way some recruiters were taught to open a sales interaction for years. But it's all wrong.

More than three decades of research tells us why. As revealed in the previous chapter, people don't always buy what they need. They usually buy what they want. How about some more examples? Do more people buy whole grain bread or white, starchy bread? Do more people buy food from a health store or go to the frozen dessert section of the grocery store?

Do your prospects always do what they need to do? Ours don't. Military recruiting organizations need sales training. However, some recruiters don't want to go through the pain required to make it effective, especially during bad economic times that usually create a target-rich recruiting environment.

Your mission is (or will be) to convince enough qualified prospects to join your branch of service. If you stop to think about it, the defense of the United States starts with every military recruiter, and that's an awesome responsibility. Obviously, that's the big picture, but you also perform your duty to provide yourself with monetary income. However, you may not want to prospect for new leads, face the embarrassment of rejection or the frustration of failure. Nevertheless, your prospects may need the opportunities you offer, but they'll only join the branch of service that offers them what they want in terms of lifestyle, benefits, length of commitment, etc.

> **Needs vs. Wants**
> What's the difference between what people need and what they want?
>
> | **Needs** | **Wants** |
> |-----------|-----------|
> | High level of awareness | Low level of awareness |
> | Fact-oriented | Emotion-based |

That's precisely why Chapter 2 recommended you start your presentation with a statement like "*My job is to help you get what you want.*" There is a big difference between what someone needs and what that person really wants. Smart recruiters know that difference and use it to their advantage.

It's All About Focus

In Chapter 1, we said people can only focus effectively on one thing at a time, yet there are four possible areas of focus in recruiting. It is possible to refine your focus even further. And this refinement will have a lot to do with your recruiting success.

As a recruiter, you are really selling only two things, no matter what opportunities your service branch can offer. You are selling *trust* and *value*. You're not selling

> **Focus:** A sharp, clearly-defined center-of-interest or expenditure of time, energy, or resources.

your ability to be a likeable person who touts every benefit your service branch offers but then fails to deliver meaningful solutions. That's the big difference between highly successful and marginally performing recruiters.

Let's look at how this works across the whole universe of recruiters. Take enough recruiters, anywhere, and you'll get a normal distribution something like this:

- 20% are not achieving, or are barely achieving, their recruiting goals
- 60% are average, or slightly above, or slightly below average
- 20% are top performers who deliver 75%-80% of the accessions in their organization

Where is your focus? What do you think drives a recruiter's success? Skills? Attitude? Professional knowledge? Luck? No, it's none of these. The major driver is a recruiter's focus.

Recruiters in the bottom 20% focus far differently than those in the top 20%. Struggling recruiters are concerned primarily about themselves and their survival. They worry about whether their recruiting career will last to the end of the month,

Where Do You Fit?
You could be heading for the bottom 20% of recruiters if your focus is on yourself, your survival or just making the minimum accession goals. The bottom 20% have a focus that says, *"I don't know if I can do this,"* or *"I don't want to do this,"* or *"Recruiting isn't right for me,"* or *"If I just make enough calls...,"* or *"If I can do enough to get by, I'll be fine."*

quarter, fiscal year, tour-of-duty or until retirement.

The middle 60% focus most of their attention on the recruiting opportunity, or their own career advancement, or perhaps their own ego, and that includes the recognition and awards that go along with being a successful recruiter.

The top 20%, however, have a very different focus. To these recruiters, it's all about the prospect. Of this group, 15% focus on what their prospects *need*, and the very top 5% focus on what their prospects really *want*. They're all about satisfying needs in the ways their prospects want to see them satisfied.

Where's your focus? Look at Figure 3-1 and ask yourself where you fall relative to the top recruiters.

Clarify Your Focus

To stay at the top, you need a philosophical understanding of prospect focus and a sales model that allows you to implement this philosophy on a daily basis. The IMPACT Selling System allows you to do that. It's a principles-based, prospect-

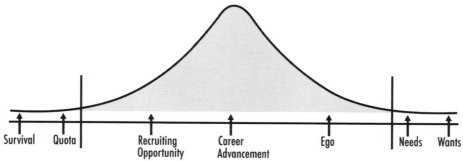

Figure 3-1: Focus and performance.

Changing Focus Endangers Your Productivity!
It's extremely easy for your focus to change because of circumstances in your career or personal life. Let's look at some examples.

How could the following circumstances force your focus to move from the prospect's needs or wants all the way back to your own survival or recruiting goals?
• Political, economic and social events that negatively impact the recruiting environment
• A long recruiting slump that jeopardizes your future as a recruiter
• A supervisor who demands rigorous reporting of phone calls, testing reports, etc.
• Financial or family issues

How about driving your focus to the recruiting opportunity, career advancement, or ego?
• A new program you are told to push but you have no knowledge about how it works
• Recruiting contests placing emphasis on selling harder to fill career fields
• Needing two more accessions by the end of the month to win a recruiting award.

Nobody said it would be easy! The irony? Focus on the prospect, and all the situations described above will not become problems.

focused, strategic process that empowers you with the selling skills necessary to keep your focus where it needs to be.

Each step of the IMPACT process has a clear and carefully-defined purpose and goal that must be understood and achieved before moving to the next step. Also, note that each step is totally prospect-focused. Now, let's look at each step in more detail.

• **Investigate** – discovering and attracting prospects who are most receptive to and need or want your recruiting opportunity.
• **Meet** – building trust and developing rapport with the most qualified prospects.
• **Probe** – asking the prospect questions to determine what they'll commit to, when they'll commit and under what conditions they'll commit.
• **Apply** – prescribing the exact application of your recruiting opportunity in ways that address your applicant's specific issues, needs, wants and desires.
• **Convince** – ensuring your prospects believe and accept what you say as being correct.
• **Tie-It-Up** – asking applicants to make a decision to commit when they are ready to do so.

The Role of Expectation

How much of your focus do you believe is driven by your self-image? How much is driven by your perception of other people in the selling and recruiting professions? Is your self-image fueled or foiled by seeing yourself as a recruiter? In other words, are you proud to call yourself a recruiter or do you use a different job title when you meet people?

IMPACT Will Sustain a Prospect-Centered Focus
Follow the IMPACT process with everyone you meet, and you'll sustain a prospect-centered focus. Moreover, you will avoid the fatal trap of focusing on yourself (survival, goal, career advancement or ego) or your organization (recruiting opportunity). Instead, you'll stay focused on your prospect's needs and wants, thus separating yourself from 80% of all other recruiters.

What if you are uncomfortable with the thought of being a recruiter? Perhaps you were assigned to this duty, and you're not a volunteer. We encourage you to think about three key concepts:

1. Set realistic, exciting objectives for yourself. Don't pressure yourself into thinking you have to be the top recruiter in your organization. Work with your supervisor to set the bar high, but not so high that it's unreachable.
2. Expand your belief system. Ignore the naysayers who say you can't succeed in your assigned territory. Military recruiting is full of true stories of recruiters who were assigned to supposedly 'dead' territories and turned them around with hard work and creativity.
3. You must see recruiting as a worthy profession. Military recruiters offer tremendous opportunities to people willing to serve their country, and it's through their work that our nation has a strong military to keep us safe and free. What's more worthy than that?

Build Your Sales Philosophy

To have a great career in recruiting, you must develop an overall philosophy of recruiting that will guide you through the good and bad times.

There is no doubt that recruiting duty can be a great career. However, top recruiters understand recruiting is all about three specific things:

*   Consistency
*   Integrity
*   Productivity that combines quantity and quality

Always aim for consistency, and you will remain a step ahead of most other recruiters. That means engaging in daily prospecting activities, always delivering high-quality, impact-driven presentations, properly servicing your influencers, prospects and applicants and being dependable, delivering on time, every time.

Maintain your integrity, and you will be known as the recruiter people can trust. Resist the temptation to disregard an applicant's self-admitted confession that contains disqualifying information on the premise that "*No one else has to know, if we both just keep quiet.*"

Recruiting large numbers of highly-qualified applicants will also differentiate you from other recruiters. Concentrate on working 'quality' prospects, and don't be a recruiter who is known for working 'anybody.' We like to say, "*Work to interest the qualified prospects; don't work to qualify the interested prospects.*" There's a fine line between the recruiter who is well-known for helping people and the

Sergeant Roberts and Sergeant Grodin

Sergeant Roberts considers himself to be a top professional recruiter. He prides himself on never processing a waiver, regardless of the prospect's circumstances. As a result, he's probably lost a few accessions over the years. The results? His enlistment packages all make it through the system quickly and smoothly. During 'easier' recruiting times, he delivered big numbers every month. However, once the United States went to war, the number of 'fully-qualified' prospects he was working dropped off dramatically. Now, Roberts is just getting by each month, but he does continue to fill the critical vacancies.

Sergeant Grodin is a very nice person. Perhaps too nice. She works some fully-qualified prospects; however, she also has desk drawers full of prospects who are overweight, medically disqualified, morally disqualified and mentally disqualified. She works long and hard submitting waivers on behalf of these prospects, and gets a fair number of 'truly deserving' ones approved. And because she is so pleasant, the applicants she does bring in are happy to refer their friends to her – even though a lot of those prospects need waivers too. Furthermore, because Grodin spends so much time on processing waivers, she usually makes her monthly goals, but can rarely place her applicants into critical career fields requiring highly-qualified people.

If you were the supervisor, which of these two would you want on your recruiting team? Isn't it a shame that we can't take a little of Sergeant Roberts and a little of Sergeant Grodin to make the ideal recruiter? However, maybe we can. That ideal recruiter could be you when you're armed with this knowledge!

'waiver king/queen' who thinks every prospect who shows an interest ought to be given the opportunity to join, regardless of their past history of law violations or illegal drug use.

Leverage Your Time, Talent, Resources and Advantage

To grow your recruiting territory and increase production, there's a three-part strategy that could redefine your recruiting career and serve you well for the rest of your life:

- *Work* to consistently recruit highly-qualified prospects.
- *Work* to service your prospects at a level that exceeds their expectations.
- *Work* to build sustained loyalty from the people you recruit and earn strong referrals from them.

Follow this strategy, and you won't be working on the wrong things. Instead, you'll be leveraging the strengths you already have. Nevertheless, to implement this action plan, you must disregard some old ways of thinking, like the old belief that says "*Under-promise and over-deliver.*" Instead, "*Promise a lot and deliver even more.*"

Furthermore, to sustain excellence, you might discover you'll have to work a little harder, longer and smarter than most other recruiters.

Asset or Enemy?

There are only four things you can do with your time: invest it, spend it, waste it or abuse it. The problem? As a recruiting professional, time is your only real inventory. It's your greatest asset if you invest

How the Three-Part Strategy Could Fail
- What happens to this strategy if you don't gain enough accessions in the first place?
- What happens if you over-promise and under-deliver?
- What happens if you can't build loyalty?
- What happens if disappointed applicants won't serve as a referral source?
- What happens if you're not willing to work hard enough to make all of this happen?

If this three-part strategy fails, it's your fault! It's not the fault of the strategy!

it wisely, and it can be your greatest enemy, if you waste or abuse it. Lots of recruiters just spend it, believing there will always be more. However, that's false logic. You can't manufacture, buy, or trade for more time. You get all there is. So, leverage your time as best you can… prospecting, selling and servicing your applicants.

Your Personal Sales Talents Audit

To maximize your talents, you must first identify the skills you already have. The most successful recruiters recognize their strengths and apply them daily. They also know their shortcomings and work to improve themselves in those areas. Furthermore, they avoid relying on their weaker talents until they have improved them to the point where they become an asset.

What Do You Do With Your Time?

Be proactive and guard your time jealously. Invest your time, don't just spend it, and avoid wasting or abusing your time at all costs. Here are some ways recruiters tend to waste or abuse time:

- Failing to prospect
- Talking to too many people superficially
- Complaining to other recruiters about their supervisor or headquarters directives and policies
- Spreading rumors and gossip
- Being disorganized
- Not confirming appointments
- Surfing the Internet

Here is a short, self-scoring audit. Please be as honest as you can about yourself. The only way to improve at anything is to have a baseline that says, "*I'm good at this and not so good at that.*" Unfortunately, people who refuse to face their challenges rarely improve.

I consider the following to be a great strength of mine:

Yes	No	N/A		
☐	☐	☐	1.	Prospecting for new business
☐	☐	☐	2.	Positioning myself as an expert
☐	☐	☐	3.	Pre-call planning for appointments and phone calls
☐	☐	☐	4.	Product knowledge
☐	☐	☐	5.	Effective travel planning
☐	☐	☐	6.	Developing internal support with school officials
☐	☐	☐	7.	Building and sustaining trust
☐	☐	☐	8.	Listening

☐	☐	☐	9. Asking strong questions
☐	☐	☐	10. Not interrupting prospects
☐	☐	☐	11. Making targeted presentations
☐	☐	☐	12. Creating and selling value
☐	☐	☐	13. Presenting the recruiting opportunity with confidence
☐	☐	☐	14. Being persuasive
☐	☐	☐	15. Finalizing transactions
☐	☐	☐	16. Satisfying applicants
☐	☐	☐	17. Delivering more than expected
☐	☐	☐	18. Selling critical career fields
☐	☐	☐	19. Gaining referrals from my satisfied applicants
☐	☐	☐	20. Sustaining meaningful relationships with key influencers
☐	☐	☐	21. Feeling good about being a recruiter

Leveraging your resources and advantages is all about maximizing the tools at your disposal. Your resources include such things as sales aids, digital equipment and professional knowledge. Advantages are the unique features of your branch of service, branding, market penetration, positioning and all the issues that make your recruiting opportunities better or more attractive than your competitors' offerings.

What Your Score Means

How did you score? If you had between 18-21 "*Yes*" answers, congratulations! You're well on your way to recruiting success. If you had 15-17 "*Yes*" answers, keep studying your craft. If you scored less than 14, you may need additional training or help from your supervisor.

What do the questions ask? The first 20 dealt with the IMPACT Selling System: questions 1-6 with the Investigate Step, questions 7-8 with the Meet Step, questions 9-10 with the Probe Step, questions 11-14 with the Apply and Convince Steps, and questions 15-20 with the Tie-It-Up Step. The final question was on how you feel about recruiting as a profession.

How did you do? What are your strengths and weaknesses? What will you do about them?

Learn to leverage what you have and you will experience even greater recruiting success. Don't worry about the things you don't have. Great recruiters don't waste time dealing with things they can't control. Instead, they concern themselves only with things they can control—and then take action with their tools and advantages.

Identifying Your Advantages

Effective recruiters are extremely knowledgeable about their resources and maximize their application every day. What resources do you have, and how effectively are you using them? Do you need more? What are they? How will you get them?

What advantages do you have in the marketplace? Is it your features and benefits? Your service's mission? The 'branding' of your service? Ease of processing? Your expertise? Are you leveraging your advantages? If not, why not? How could you do it better?

The Recruiter's Knowledge-Based Raw Materials

The best recruiters don't just work *in* their recruiting zone; they work *on* their recruiting zone. In other words, they start shaping their territory by building a strong knowledge base that includes:

- Knowing their zone
- Critical manning needs of their service
- Networking know-how
- Major employers in the area
- Competitive factors
- Geography and population density, socio-economic realities and demographics
- Being familiar with the local media

Marketplace Intelligence

Just as no two recruiters are the same, no two recruiting territories are identical. Therefore, every recruiter needs to learn as much as possible about their marketplace.

Here are a few planning questions to ask yourself:

1. What are the most effective target markets for me?
2. Which target market is traditionally most resistant to joining?
3. Which target markets are cyclical? (e.g. high school students)
4. Which target markets are most volatile? (Subject to rapid change)
5. What trends am I seeing? (e.g. Economy bad, recruiting good or vice versa)

Competitive Scouting Report

More than likely, you're not the only job opportunity in town. At the very least, you're competing with other military recruiters in the same markets for the same people. How much do you know about your competition? As Michael Corleone said in the movie, *The Godfather Part II, "Keep your friends close, and your enemies closer."* Now we're not saying other recruiters from other branches are your enemy, but we think you get the point. Here are eight questions you should find the answers to, if you want to compete successfully against other military recruiting organizations:

1. Who are the toughest competitors in my zone?
2. What is the sales and marketing philosophy of my toughest competitors?
3. Who is the recruiter (by name) I compete against most often? Strengths? Weaknesses? Selling Philosophy? Experience?
4. In comparison to my organization, how is their service component positioned in the marketplace? (Stronger or weaker?)
5. Do our competitors have glitches we can exploit?
6. Do we have glitches our competitors can exploit?
7. What is their incentive history?
8. How do their incentive programs compare to ours?

Checklist for Chapter 3

☐ Your prospect may need the opportunities you offer, but they'll only join the branch of service that offers them what they want in terms of lifestyle, benefits, length of commitment, etc.

☐ Needs have a high level of awareness and are fact-oriented. Wants have a low level of awareness and are emotion-based.

☐ Focus is a sharp, clearly-defined center of influence or expenditure of time, energy or dollars.

☐ You are really selling only two things: trust and value.

☐ The bottom 20% of recruiters focus on survival or goal. The middle 60% focus on the recruiting opportunity, career advancement or their ego. The top 20% of recruiters focus on the needs and wants of their prospects.

☐ The IMPACT Selling System is a principles-based, customer-focused, strategic process that will empower you with the selling skills necessary to keep your focus where it needs to be:
   • Investigate—discovering and attracting qualified prospects.
   • Meet—building trust and developing rapport.
   • Probe—asking strong questions to determine what your applicant is looking for.

- Apply—prescribing the exact solution your applicant needs and wants.
- Convince—proving what you say is true.
- Tie-It-Up—asking prospects to commit and servicing after the sale.

☐ Three specific things will help you build your sales philosophy: consistency, integrity and productivity that combines quantity and quality.

☐ Three-part sales success strategy: consistently recruit highly qualified prospects, service your applicants at levels that exceed their expectations and build sustained loyalty from the people you recruit to earn strong referrals from them.

☐ Four things you can do with time: invest, spend, waste or abuse it.

☐ Build a strong knowledge base about your recruiting territory, gather marketplace intelligence and scout your competition.

Chapter 4
The Investigate Step (Part I) – Positioning

Investigate: To gather sufficient information about your zone, target markets and individual prospects within them to enable you to make the best possible presentation.

The Investigate Step of the IMPACT Selling System is divided into three parts, and the first is Positioning. Prospects and influencers pay attention to recruiters they believe have something important to say to them. That's why your positioning is so critical to your recruiting success.

Ask yourself this question: How much do the people in my recruiting zone know about me, my recruiting opportunities and the branch of service I represent? Furthermore, if they do know of me, what are they thinking and saying about me, my recruiting opportunities and my service branch?

The real issue is not how often you tell your story. The secret is when you tell it, how you are positioned when you tell it, and how often you tell it to the right people. It's the difference between looking everywhere for opportunities and creating your own opportunities.

There's an old adage in recruiting that says: *"It's not important who you know. It's important who knows you!"* What does that mean? Simply this: you need to create a presence, awareness and recognition in the minds of your prospects and influencers that make them think of you first and most receptively when it's time for them to make a decision about joining or recommending to someone that they contact you.

> ### Personal Positioning
> How your prospects and applicants perceive you relative to all other military recruiters and career opportunities they may be interested in pursuing. It's also presence, awareness and recognition.
>
> What should the goal of your personal positioning be? That's easy. Be the first and best choice in the minds of your prospects and influencers. Here are some examples of how you can position yourself:
>
> - Career counselor
> - Successful testimonial
> - Military expert
> - Advocate
> - Creative problem solver

The Power of Personal Positioning

To become the recruiter of choice, there are several actions you must take. These measures are critical because your prospects have many options in today's highly-competitive recruiting marketplace.

This power of personal positioning is a weapon with great potential, but only if you choose to use it. It can crush your competition. Take a page from the powerful marketing strategies of well-positioned companies and put the strength of positioning on your side.

Personal positioning is all about three things:

1. Perception
2. Choice
3. Primacy

It's creating a perception in your territory that you are everywhere. It's making your target segments believe that you and your branch of service are the top choice, and they would be foolish not to do business with you. And it's all about you being the recruiter they hear from or about first, last and always—the expert. With the magic of digital tools and the accuracy to identify your specific market, all of this is possible. Remember this: to your prospects, your personal positioning can supersede the positioning of your branch of service—because to them you are the military organization you represent. But you have to create the image you want them to have of you.

Ten Ways to Better Positioning

Let's examine ten things you can do to position yourself as an expert:

1. Research organizations your influencers belong to and join them.
2. Write articles about recruiting opportunities for publication in local, school and military newspapers.
3. Read magazines and other informative materials your prospects and influencers read.
4. Search the Web for information related to your target markets and influencers.
5. Gather as much information as you can about your competition.
6. Ask other recruiters what they see going on—what trends they see, what the most common questions they're asked are, how they are serving their applicants better, etc.
7. Conduct center-of-influence events and serve as the guest speaker.
8. Offer to sponsor or serve as a judge at Junior ROTC drill meets.
9. Serve on appropriate boards and committees that have high visibility with target prospects or community leaders.
10. Work harder and smarter than your competition.

These strategies are all doable and used successfully by recruiters all over the country. There's only one question. Do you see any value in them? If you do, then the only remaining issue is whether or not you'll put in the time and effort required to turn ideas into realities.

Seven Ways to Misposition Yourself

Do you think it's possible to misposition yourself in your recruiting zone? Absolutely! Here are seven ways it

Don't Do It All

Don't try to implement all ten positioning strategies at once. You're far better off employing one or two activities you want to undertake and have success with those than to have marginal results doing ten things poorly.

Decide which activities would work best in your territory, and determine if you have the expertise and commitment to do them. If you don't have the know-how, study, learn or seek out others to help you. That's easy. Now, are you ready to make the commitment?

could happen, and if you do any of these things, you'll have trouble finding fully qualified prospects, producing enough accessions or building a good reputation. Avoid these mistakes:

1. Too much cold calling
2. Appearing as a pest to your prospects
3. Coming across as too desperate to gain an accession
4. Behaving like a stereotypical, fast-talking recruiter
5. Portraying yourself as the '*waiver king*' or '*queen*'
6. Being a '*benefits-dumper*'
7. Selling jobs before qualifying the prospect

Let's cover how each of these mistakes can damage your efforts:

Too much cold calling. Although some cold calling may be necessary either early in your recruiting career, or if you transfer to a new territory, smart recruiters do all they can to abandon this strategy as quickly as possible. Not only is cold calling tough to do every day, the chances of uncovering qualified prospects through this method are very slim. If you don't believe me, go back and review the five characteristics of a qualified prospect. Next, ask yourself what are the chances of randomly calling someone and finding out they possess all five.

Cold Calling
Making phone calls, drop-in visits or any other type of uninvited solicitation on prospects or influencers about whom you know very little and who have no idea about you, your branch of service or your recruiting opportunities.

Another problem with cold calling is it positions you as a recruiter who is desperate for business and whose opportunities aren't in great demand. The other person thinks, "*Don't you have anything better to do with your time?*"

Appearing as a pest to your prospects. There's a fine line between being persistent and being a pest. Think about that for a minute. What would you think of a recruiter who kept calling you incessantly? Would you see that person as a professional whose expertise and time are valuable or as an unpleasant nuisance who simply doesn't get the message to stop bothering you?

Coming across as too desperate to gain an accession. There will be times when your personal focus shifts from the prospect to yourself because you feel the pressure to make your mission. However, you must never give your prospects that impression. That's tough to do. However, letting the whole world know you're so desperate is a fatal error.

Fitting the stereotype of the fast-taking recruiter. Let's face it. There are stereotypes for any profession or group of people, including military recruiters. But being labeled as a backslapping, approval-seeking, fast-talking recruiter is not going to position you as a powerful professional.

Portraying yourself as a '*waiver king* or '*queen.' Recruiters who work unqualified prospects have only one way to go in their careers—out of it. What do we mean? Recruiting is more than just volume; it's also about quality. Top producers position themselves as solution-providers, professionals who work with qualified prospects, not as social workers who are willing to take a chance on anybody. Waiver kings and queens, as a rule, have a short life in recruiting. They stay competitive until they can't keep up with all the paperwork or the extra effort required chasing down prospects that are technically unqualified to begin with. Don't join them.

Being a '*benefits dumper.' Truth be told, your prospects aren't interested in every benefit military service offers. Instead, they're attracted to a few specific features they believe will provide the solutions they want. Consequently, your task is to find out exactly what your prospects are seeking. Is it education? Training? Income? Prestige? Pride? Patriotism? Advancement? You also need to know how the features of the recruiting opportunities in your arsenal will provide answers to whatever problems your prospects are trying to solve or goals they're hoping to achieve. Unfortunately, some recruiters don't make the effort to narrow down each prospect's interests. Instead of asking questions, they recite a litany of features in hopes they'll hit on something the prospect wants. It's sort of like the car salesperson who fails to ask what you want in a new car. Instead, he/she starts with the car's headlights and walks around the entire vehicle giving you a short speech on each feature. Besides not being interested in every element, you won't remember what the salesperson talked about anyway. It's information overload.

Selling jobs before qualifying the prospect. Let's face it, even though every military job is important and offers great benefits, some career fields/occupational specialties have more 'appeal' than others. And chances are you will occasionally meet prospects interested in just one job, because they think it's the one they really want. Unfortunately, you won't always have openings in those 'desirable' career fields, or your prospect may not meet all the educational, physical or moral standards that go along with some jobs. However, some recruiters, in their zeal to please a prospect, 'sell' the job instead of building value for the overall opportunity. Then, when the prospect learns he or she can't have a specific job, they lose interest in committing.

How to Position Yourself as an Expert

There's no secret here. To position yourself as an expert, you must become a recruiting expert. But what things do you need to be an authority about? Start with the features of your branch of service. However, information about what you can offer means far more than having just 'technical' knowledge about each feature.

Trade Secrets
Sharp recruiters position themselves in ways consistent with the image of their branch of service. That means you need to be very careful about things like your dress, personal hygiene, neatness, punctuality, grammar and even ensuring your business cards are clean, have no bent edges and have no notes or writing of any sort on the back!

It also means you're an expert in the following areas:

- Your service branch's mission and history
- The future outlook of your service branch
- How your prospects stand to benefit in light of current opportunities and future trends

Product Knowledge
It's not how much you know about your branch of service. Instead, it's how good you are at accessing what you know and then stating that information in terms that are meaningful and relevant to your prospects.

Dress, Style & Image

For every recruiter, image is critical. In fact, your appearance in uniform is the most important positioning tool you have. This includes your haircut, shoeshine, ribbons and badges. And don't forget your hat (or beret). To our knowledge, no branch of service has deemed its '*cover*' optional for recruiters. You may think that when you're a long way from a military facility no one notices or cares if you wear a hat. However, there are people, particularly veterans, who know the hat is part of the uniform, and if you're not going to wear it, what else are you not doing that you're supposed to? It's a matter of integrity. And don't try to tell yourself the primary reason you don't wear your hat is because you think people won't join if they think they have to wear a hat. The fact is the hat is part of the uniform, so let them get used to it now.

But here's another question. What is the right uniform to wear? Should you always wear a tie or tab? Do you need a service coat on every school visit? You have to be the judge. If you're visiting a high school, and it's hot outside, you probably ought to go with an open collar. But what if your meeting is with a college dean? You probably should dress a little more formal. And what if you're not sure? Call ahead and ask the receptionist or the person you're going to meet with about the dress standard. If everyone is in a business suit, you should wear your comparable uniform. Asking about the dress code will not be perceived as a strange or stupid question. If anything, you'll win points for demonstrating respect.

How to Dress Like a Pro

Top recruiters wear the appropriate uniform in every situation. And they do their best to come across as professional, but not intimidating. Every aspect of their appearance, from shoes to hair, is meticulous and sends a message of having pride in what they do and respect for the service they represent. Sharp-looking recruiters position themselves as military professionals and consultative experts who know the importance of respect, style and image.

Double-check everything before you leave your office. This includes fact sheets, sales aids and tools, pens, business cards and every facet of your appearance.

Nothing looks worse than reaching into your briefcase for a business card or to show your prospect a brochure only to discover it's not there. Worse yet, how about handing out a business card that's wrinkled, torn or has writing on the back? How do these errors position you in someone's eyes? We both know; they're thinking about calling another recruiter!

Positioning yourself correctly, however, can also be an 'inside' job. Let's look at what that means.

The Role of Self Image and Positioning Yourself

Self image is essential to your success. Truthfully, you will never achieve any more in your career or life than your self-image will allow you.

Sergeant Wilson and Petty Officer Grayson

Sergeant Wilson and Petty Officer Grayson have been friendly, and sometimes unfriendly, competitors in the same recruiting territory for several years. They often compete with each other in the non-prior service enlisted market. Unfortunately for Wilson, he loses about 80% of the time when one of his prospects also talks to Petty Officer Grayson. And he can't figure out why.

Wilson believes befriending all his prospects and pushing the latest incentive programs his service has to offer is the shortest route to an accession. His office and government car are usually a mess. His uniforms are faded and worn, and he knows very little about the recruiting opportunities offered by the other services. When prospects or influencers ask him questions he doesn't know the answers to, he simply recommends they search his service's Website.

On the other hand, Grayson sells the outcomes her prospects are trying to achieve. She focuses on providing valuable, targeted information to her prospects, applicants and influencers, and she displays a persona consistent with the image of her organization. To the people she meets, she is the service she represents. Grayson also works hard to educate people about the tangible and intangible benefits of military service, and there's hardly a fact about her branch she doesn't know off the top of her head. Furthermore, if she doesn't have an answer, she finds the right one and calls each person back promptly with the information.

Does Grayson know something Wilson doesn't? Why do you think Wilson loses 80% of the time?

Remember when people said positive things to you earlier in your life? "*You'll be highly successful,*" or "*You show great promise.*" How about the opposite? "*You'll never amount to anything,*" or "*You'll never be as successful as your sisters.*"

Self Image

The impression you have developed of yourself through experiences, through things people have said to you or about you and everything you have read, understood, or believed about yourself—good or bad.

How can you position yourself for success when you don't see yourself as capable of achievement? Let's take it a step further. How do you position yourself as a professional recruiter when a common perception of military recruiters is sometimes less than stellar? What if you share that view?

Consider this question: How do you establish yourself as a professional in your own mind if you are expected to recruit in a slick, outdated way, using memorized phrases, handling objections with tricky maneuvers or gaining commitment with questionable tactics? You know that answer too.

To position yourself for success, you must believe in yourself. You must also think recruiting duty is an honorable profession. Then you must also trust that your service's recruiting opportunity is the most viable, valuable and logical choice your prospects could ever make. It takes a special person to hang in there when times get tough. And that person is you, isn't it?

Checklist for Chapter 4

☐ Investigate: To gather sufficient information about your zone, target markets and individual prospects within them to enable you to make the best possible presentation.

☐ Personal positioning is creating a presence, awareness, and recognition in the minds of your prospects and influencers. It's all about three things:
  • Perception
  • Choice
  • Primacy

☐ Make use of some of the 10 ways to better positioning, and avoid the ways some recruiters traditionally misposition themselves.

☐ Position yourself in ways consistent with the image of your branch of service.

☐ It's not how much you know about your branch of service. Instead, it's how good you are at accessing what you know and then stating that information in terms that are meaningful and relevant.

☐ Dress appropriately for every situation, and present a professional military image.

☐ Prior to an appointment, double-check everything. This includes sales aids and tools, pens, business cards and every facet of your dress.

☐ Self image is crucial. You will never achieve any more success in your recruiting career or your life than your self image will allow you.

Chapter 5
The Investigate Step (Part 2) –
Prospecting

Investigate: To gather sufficient information about your zone, target markets and individual prospects within them to enable you to make the best possible presentation.

The second part of the Investigate Step of the IMPACT Selling System is the physical activity of traditional prospecting.

The Difference Between Suspects and Qualified Prospects

Nothing is more important to your recruiting success than the science and art of prospecting. Prospecting is a science because certain universal principles guide its processes. It's also an art because prospecting requires a carefully-defined set of skills to succeed.

Your recruiting accessions will be directly proportional to the number of qualified prospects you're in front of on a consistent basis. On the other hand, when recruiters fail, they generally fail for one reason: not enough qualified prospects. To be an effective prospector, you must first identify the segments of your niche market that have a sufficient supply of suspects with the potential to become qualified prospects.

Niche Market: A group of people who might be interested in and qualified to join your service branch.

Suspect: A person…
1. With whom you've opened communication;
2. Who may have a need you can satisfy, although he or she may not know it;
3. Who may or may not have the ability to qualify or the authority to commit;
4. Who may or may not have any sense of urgency about committing to your recruiting opportunity;
5. Who may or may not be willing to listen to you.

Segment: A specific set of suspects containing people who may or may not qualify as prospects, and they fall within the general niche you recruit into. Within your niche market, there are target segments you recruit into. For example, you may prospect for enlisted non-prior service suspects, enlisted prior-service suspects, non-prior service line officer suspects, prior-service line officer prospects, non-prior service health professions suspects, prior-service health professions prospects, etc. Good prospectors segment their niche and then prospect each segment differently.

The secret to successful prospecting is to be in front of qualified prospects when they're ready to make a commitment. Be aware that people generally move from the suspect stage to the qualified prospect stage on their own time schedule, not on yours. You need to either be there or be the one they think of first when that happens.

Part of this secret is to be the most visible option for your prospects. By targeting your efforts in specific segments, you increase the probability of becoming the recruiter of choice for the people who fit in those segments.

Qualified Prospects
In Chapter 2, we said qualified prospects exhibit five common traits:
1. The have a need for what you offer and are aware of it.
2. They have both the authority to make the decision and ability to qualify for the opportunity.
3. The have a relative sense of urgency about the decision.
4. They trust you and your branch of service.
5. They are willing to listen to you.

The Three Most Essential Prospecting Principles

Three principles applied consistently can help your prospecting:

#1 The better job you do of finding and attracting qualified prospects, the higher your closing average will be.

Look back at those five characteristics of a qualified prospect and ask yourself, *"If all my prospects met those criteria, could I convince most of them to join?"* What does your answer tell you about the people you're currently working or, perhaps, should be working?

#2 Your future success in recruiting is in direct proportion to the quality and breadth of your prospect file.

The truth should be obvious. However, some things aren't so cut and dried. For example, what does 'quality' really mean? Simply this: prospects with all five characteristics of a qualified prospect who think of you first are the highest-quality prospects. What about breadth? It means you must be active and highly-visible in a target segment to support your recruiting efforts or be active in enough segments with sufficient pools of qualified prospects necessary to sustain satisfactory production.

When you have enough quality prospects, your recruiting career is in good hands. However, if you fail to accomplish that objective, you will struggle. It's that simple.

3¢
USA

ILLUSTRATION

Sergeant Thomas and Sergeant Packer
Sergeant Thomas was the top recruiter in his organization, year in and year out, good times or bad times for military recruiting – it made no difference. Sergeant Packer, a rookie recruiter, was curious how Thomas did it. One day Packer asked the inevitable question of Thomas, *"How do you do it?"* Packer expected Thomas to say he needed to be front of three or four people to gain one accession, but that wasn't the answer he heard.

Here's what Thomas said, *"My closing ratio is in direct proportion to the number of qualified prospects I'm in front of. And then it depends on how good I am when I'm in front of the right ones."*

Words of wisdom from a great recruiter, and his wall full of plaques proved his insight worked.

#3 The recruiter who asks enough of the right questions of the right people, in the right places, will always have plenty of qualified prospects.

What questions must you ask? They're easy to remember and just like the questions investigative reporters are trained to ask: Who? What? When? Where? Why? How?

"*Why?*" questions help you prioritize your time, as you determine the process prospects use to move from suspect to qualified prospect status.

'*What?*' questions are extremely valuable with your most qualified prospects, since they help you focus on the specific issues your applicant is interested in discussing.

Timing could be a recruiter's most underutilized tool. Perhaps you're guilty of the same error. For example, it's poor practice to set up appointments that are convenient for you but inconvenient for your prospect. Also, be sure you don't get so short on prospects that you'll jump at any appointment whenever you can get one, no matter how weak it might be. The best strategy is blending your circum-

Helpful "Why?" Questions

- Why would this prospect be in a position to decide to commit now?
- Why might he/she resist committing at this point?
- Why would my present timing be especially good or bad?
- Why might I get a particularly good (or bad) hearing now?
- Why would my recruiting opportunity be particularly appealing?
- Why might it be unappealing?

Useful "What?" Questions

- What will this prospect find most attractive about our recruiting opportunity?
- What might this prospect find least attractive?
- What should I do to get this prospect's attention?
- What do I need to know about this person? Their family? Their preferences for making a commitment?
- What will be my objective for the first call?
- What do I have to do to get an appointment?

Productive "When?" Questions

- When is the best time for me to prospect? When is the time I am at my best?
- When is the most likely time I will be able to make contact with this prospect? When is the least likely? When is this prospect's schedule probably the lightest? Most hectic?
- When should I contact this prospect again if my first attempt fails?

> ### "How?" Questions That Work
>
> - How can I prospect more productively without hurting my face-to-face interviewing time?
> - How can I improve my prospecting skills?
> - How can I maximize my skills in approaching tough prospects?
> - How can I follow up on every prospect more effectively?

stances with those of the prospect, so you'll both win.

"*How?*" questions are the most critical for you in your prospecting success. You'll find a lot of your "*How?*" answers will spring from other questions.

What Are Your Chances?

Our observations from working in the private sector indicate salespeople have a far better chance of selling current customers more of their products or services, about a 1:2 chance. They generally have about a 1:4 chance of selling to a referral or a customer they've done 'business' with some time in the past – and a very poor 1:14 chance of selling to someone they've never dealt with before.

What do those numbers tell you? You need lots of qualified prospects if you're starting out fresh with no existing customers or a weak referral base. It also tells you it's far easier to sell to existing customers or referrals than to prospects who barely know you. Finally, it tells you it's far more expensive, time-consuming, and gut-wrenching to fight your way through those 1:14's than it is to work with the easier 1:2 and 1:4 ratios.

We mentioned those statistics apply to the private sector. Even if the ratios don't match up exactly, do you think there are similar patterns in military recruiting? For example, can you think of any prospects that might fit into the 1:2 category? How about prospects who are still on active duty, but their enlistment or commitment is about to expire? If you're trying to recruit them, how would you rate your chances? After all, they really are already doing 'business' with the military, and they meet many of the five characteristics of a qualified prospect, don't they?

Who do you think might fit into the 1:4 category? Most likely it's your prior-service prospects who left active duty or the active reserve within the last couple of years. They may even be in the Individual Ready Reserve (IRR), but they haven't worn a uniform in a while. You know that these prospects have also '*bought*' at least one military commitment and might be convinced to join again.

And those 1:14 prospects? You probably guessed—those are non-prior service prospects. You'll have to talk to, test and physical quite a few before you find one who will make it all the way through the recruiting pipeline.

Yes, it is tougher to work the non-prior service market; however, no matter how tough and time-consuming these prospects might be, they make up a significant portion of the people your service branch must recruit to fill its ranks, and you'll most likely have to do business with them.

Two Conditions of Getting Referrals

To obtain referrals from your applicants, two conditions are essential. First, they must be more than satisfied; they must be thrilled with you, your branch of service and the recruiting opportunities you provided. Second, you must ask them properly for a referral. A common question we receive is *"When is the right time to ask for a referral?"* Here's the answer: *"It's when you've earned the right to do so."* For some applicants, it could be when you offer them the recruiting opportunity they were hoping for. For others, it might be the day they enlist or receive a commission. And for some, it might be as late as when they return from their initial military training or technical training school.

We don't recommend trying to 'perpetuate' off prospects the first time you meet them. Far too many recruiters do this—primarily because they've been told to do it by their supervisors, and they get counseled or reprimanded if they don't ask for names. Just for a moment, put yourself in the position of the prospect or 'buyer.' If you're at a car dealership buying a vehicle or at an electronics store purchasing a big-screen, high-definition television, how do you feel about the salesperson saying to you, *"How about giving me the names of three of your friends who I could talk to?"* Doesn't it create the impression that the salesperson is now more interested in these other three people than you? Furthermore, before you've bought and used that product, you may know nothing about how well it will perform or if the follow-up service will be satisfactory. Do you really feel comfortable giving out the names of your friends? Suppose you do give out those names and after buying the product you have a bad experience with the merchant and your friends do too. Now how are you going to feel? On the other hand, if you make a major purchase, and you're satisfied that every promise was kept, don't you feel more comfortable making a recommendation?

Referrals are the best way to find new prospects; however, referrals from satisfied applicants are the way to go. You may have to wait a little longer to get that referral, but you'll find its quality well worth the time.

What Smart Recruiters Always Know

- What qualified prospects they're currently working with
- How many qualified prospects they have at any point in time
- Which stage of the selling process each prospect is in
- When the prospect will most likely agree to commit

"Who?" questions are among the most valuable prospecting tools, because they help you identify the people you want to work with. To do this, there is a series of questions you should ask yourself. However, before doing that, identify the specific segments you want to attack. For example, are you going after the non-prior service or prior service target segments? Officer or enlisted? Line or medical?

Finding Your Target with "Who?" Questions

- Who are ideal prospects I can contact right now?
- Who are some former prospects I can contact?
- Who are some former prospects who may be more qualified now than they were before?
- Who do I know who might lead me to some ideal prospects?
- Who do I know who has the most influence on the prospects I'm able to identify?

It may seem like we have been dealing with lots of questions. However, remember prospecting and selling are about the questions you ask and not the talking you do! And the most important questions are the ones you should first ask yourself. These questions will aim you in the right direction and provide the answers to help you proceed with the confidence and clarity you need to become a great prospector.

Here are a few more questions to ask yourself:

- *When is the best day of the week to contact prospects of certain types?*
  - For example, you might find that certain people are never available on Fridays; others might be easier to reach in the evenings or on weekends, etc.
- *When can you get the most attentive hearing?*

- Are your prospects busier in the morning or the afternoon, for example?
- *How does each prospect prefer to be contacted? Phone? Email? Text message?*
- *When are you at your personal selling best?*
- *Are you a 'morning' or 'afternoon' person?*

Effective prospecting means finding ideal prospects. There are lots of sources, and you should choose which ones you prefer to use.

There are lots of things you can do to raise your visibility. You can send standard or electronic birthday cards, seasonal greetings or congratulatory notes at graduation time. You can also send prospects and influencers pertinent newspaper clippings, article reprints or newsletters about subjects of interest to them. Your goal is for prospects and influencers to hear from you several times per year.

Four Ways to Stay Organized

Try doing these four specific things:

- Use the *Parthenon* approach for planning your prospecting activities. (See sidebar)
- Use your applicant-tracking system for storing data. Every service branch has one, and we're sure it's standard operating procedure to use it.
- Create a tickler file or use a digital reminder system to stay in touch with prospects at the right times.
- Use frequent contact tools (e-mails, newsletters, letters, calls, text messages, cards, etc.) to keep you at the top of each prospect's mind. The same goes for keeping in touch with key influencers.

Approaching Your Prospect

Approaching prospects is one of the most difficult steps in prospecting. How will you open the conversation? How will the prospect respond?

There are two keys to prospecting correctly. The first, as we've discussed, is your positioning. The second is having every tool you'll need for the appointment. That's something we'll discuss in the next chapter.

The Parthenon Approach to Prospecting

Organize your prospecting efforts by building a Parthenon. The idea is taken from the ancient Greek structure. The building's roof contains a segment of prospects you want to recruit into. For example: Non-Prior Service Enlisted. The columns holding up the roof contain the strategies you can employ to search for non-prior service enlisted prospects. Why so many columns? What if one of your strategies doesn't work? If one or two pillars crack, the whole building will not collapse. The strategies in the remaining pillars can still help you to succeed. Below the pillars, place the 'tactical' steps you must complete to implement each prospecting strategy.

Here's a sample Parthenon. Your strategies could look similar or different, depending on your recruiting territory. Why? Because no two recruiting zones are exactly alike. A strategy that works well in one recruiter's location may not work as well in another's zone.

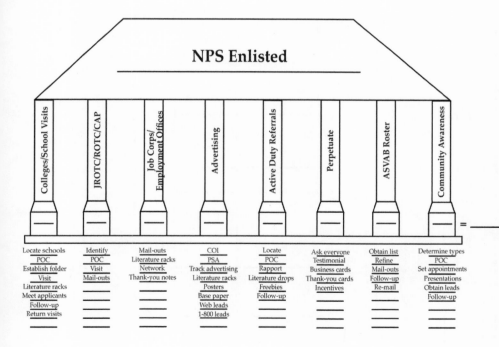

Blank Parthenon

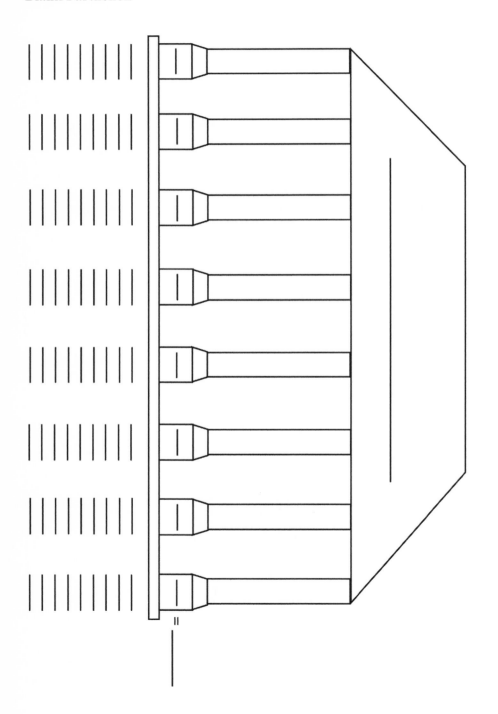

To quickly capture your prospect's interest, there are several things you can do. For example, arrange an introduction from a mutual contact or influencer, such as a school counselor, coach or member of the business community. You can arrange to meet them in person or you can contact them by phone. We'll have more on this tactic later.

Where Do You Find Prospects?

Before you can talk to a prospect, you've got to find them. The sources you identify depend entirely on which target segments you're recruiting into. Here are a few ways you can gather data.

The Value of Your Accessions May Be Far More Than You Think It Is

Don't be afraid to ask people you've already recruited for help. If you provided great value, they'll want to refer you to others. In fact, most armed services sponsor recognition and rewards programs for members who refer prospects to a recruiter. Always remember there's potential long-term value to be gained from every applicant, once you've gotten them to commit. What might they be worth over the course of years in terms of referrals and good-will? Therefore, never take any of the people you recruit for granted.

Don't ignore the best source of prospects you have—the people you've already recruited. They know people just like themselves with similar interests. What schools did these people attend? Where do they work? What organizations or associations do they belong to?

It May Not Be Easy

If you replace a recruiter who is transferring out of your territory, his or her applicants could be an excellent source to help you get started. Your first step should be to contact these people. Make the point of the call to simply introduce yourself and explain how you are prepared to answer any questions or provide additional assistance in processing for enlistment or commissioning. If the prospects or applicants are happy, they'll welcome your call. However; if they aren't happy, you may hear some negative reactions. Some people may feel they were abandoned once the recruiter found out he or she was leaving. And, unfortunately, sometime that's true. The outgoing recruiter, especially if they left under adverse conditions, may have failed to deliver the quality service the applicant expected and deserved. In some cases you may have a tough time finding some of your predecessor's prospects or applicants. Why? People move or switch jobs and the recruiter failed to keep up with the changes.

School lists, ASVAB (Armed Services Vocational Aptitude Battery) rosters, association registers, IRR (Individual Ready Reserve) rosters, DMDC (Defense Manpower Data Center) and ETS (Estimated Time to Separation) rosters are also good sources of prospects.

You should also consider prescribing to specialized publications, Websites or blogs containing information for veterans or people who might be interested in joining the military.

Discovering Acres of Diamonds

Sergeant Rickey was a recruiter for a reserve component unit located on an active duty base. Each time the base held its Newcomers Briefings for arriving active duty personnel and their dependents, Rickey was a featured speaker. He knew from personal experience that many active duty military people were married to former active duty military members who separated from active duty either to raise children or because the couple could no longer get stationed together. Rickey explained to the audience that his reserve unit had plenty of great part-time jobs, and by 'returning' to the active reserve, a person could usually get back their former rank, make an excellent part-time wage, volunteer to work extra 'mandays' to earn more money and build credit toward a retirement program. Furthermore, since some of the spouses were still in the IRR (Remember the 1:4 ratio?), accessing them was a breeze.

The Telephone

Sooner or later, you're going to need to contact your prospects, and the telephone remains the best tool for that task. Some argument could be made for text messaging or e-mail, particularly with today's younger, tech-savvy prospects. However, you must avoid spamming. Not only is spamming illegal, the people you're trying to contact will find you very annoying.

Information Is Everywhere, If You Look For It

Various publications and Websites can provide information about changes in your community, important educational trends, personnel changes and more. Check out these publications and visit the Websites of the schools and businesses in your territory to look for announcements of promotions, personnel changes, awards, etc. Call the person who's listed as the contact. Congratulate people who are mentioned: we'll bet you're one of the few who'll do that. What if they are potential prospects or influencers? Who will they remember?

Consider using a pre-approach letter or series of mailings. Also, be sure to include a direct response mechanism that allows people to respond with minimal effort on their part. That way, when you do call them, it's justifiable, because you're responding to their request.

There are few things more distressing than a full day of telephone cold calling as you refine a list of suspects or prospects. Ideally, you should only be responding to qualified prospects who sincerely want to talk with you.

Things to Avoid When Telephone Prospecting

Don't make these mistakes:

- Making one call and then stopping for a break.
- Counting a busy signal as a completed call.
- Failing to call back after leaving one voice-mail message.
- Fiddling with papers, paper clips, pencils, pens or your computer between calls.

Here are a few more important points. Ask the prospect's permission to talk and then quickly give your prospect a reason to listen to you. For example, try using a Direct Value Statement to position yourself and your service branch. A Direct Value Statement is simply a short speech to position yourself and deliver a free, 15 to 30 second commercial for your service branch. It should communicate the fundamental reason for both you and your organization's existence. A pre-prepared and rehearsed statement lets you quickly get to the point of a face-to-face or telephone conversation or to leave an effective voice mail.

Here's an example: *"We assist people like you to find rewarding careers in the (Your Branch of Service) where they can enjoy many tangible and intangible benefits and expand their personal experiences. We do this by conducting an interview where we discuss your interests and qualifications and then attempt to match you with opportunities that will help you achieve your personal goals."*

You will often encounter three distinct scenarios when telephone prospecting, and here's how you handle each one correctly:

- **You place a call to a prospect.** We're assuming you previously sent some informational materials to the prospect. Cold-calling is difficult enough; however, it's even tougher when you haven't '*warmed*' the call by sending out a letter or brochure ahead of time. When your prospect answers the phone, start the conversation by saying the person's name and introducing yourself. For example. *"Hello Jane. My name is _____ with the (Your*

branch of service)." Next, ask the prospect if he/she has a moment to talk
with you. If the prospect agrees to speak, say your Direct Value Statement
and then ask the prospect if he/she received the materials you sent.

- **You're calling a referral.** Say, *"Hello Jane. My name is* _____
  with the (Your branch of service). Bob Danberry, a mutual friend of ours,
  asked *me to give you a call, and I* ***promised*** *him I would."* The keywords are
  *"**asked**"* and *"**promised**,"* and they will almost always cause the prospect to
  listen to what you have to say. This is an excellent time to use your Direct
  Value Statement to further position yourself and your branch of service.

- **You call and get voicemail.** Say, *"Hello Jane. My name is* _____
  with the (Your branch of service)." Next, insert your Direct Value Statement,
  and then add a brief message similar to the following: *"The purpose of my
  call is to see if there is some way that I might be of service to you. Should you
  wish to call me back, I would like to leave my phone number."* Leave your
  number twice, and say it slow enough for the prospect to be able to write it
  down as they listen to the message. Now add, *"If I don't hear from you in a
  day or two, I will certainly give you a call back to see if there is some way
  we might be able to get together."* When do you quit? Here are the facts. If
  you call someone three times and there's no response or you have no luck
  getting to him or her, your prospect is saying *"I'm not interested now."* It
  does not necessarily mean he or she won't be interested later. Your job is to
  stay in touch with these future prospects. And you can do so electronically,
  with mailings, news clippings, etc.—all the things we've been talking about
  throughout this entire book.

Prospecting will always be critical to your recruiting success, even though there
may be times, particularly during a bad economy, when it seems you have plenty
of leads (but not necessarily qualified leads). However, the ways you initially
position yourself will ultimately define how receptive your prospects will be to
dealing with you. Furthermore, it doesn't end there. Now you must properly plan
for your face-to-face interviews to maximize your chances of gaining the accession.

But, before we go there, remember your primary prospecting goal – to sell an
appointment.

Selling an Appointment

How do you sell an appointment? Let's examine the process in detail. When telephone prospecting, keep the conversation focused and moving toward an appointment. Unfortunately, not all prospects are easy to keep on track. You'll encounter

objections, and they may refuse to set appointments. Occasionally people might just hang-up because they have no interest in joining or have no respect for the military. Don't take the rejection personally. They don't know you well enough to reject you; instead, they're rejecting what they think you represent.

What are the most common reasons why prospects raise objections to making an appointment? First, and foremost, is a poorly-designed approach. You can solve that by understanding one simple thing. Your goal is to sell an appointment – period – nothing more and nothing less. In the IMPACT System, positioning, prospecting and pre-call planning all occur in the Investigate Step, and those activities are designed to prepare you for the Meet Step. However, there's a valuable secret we will share. When selling an appointment, you are also meeting and probing your prospect on the telephone. Those two steps also briefly occur inside the Investigate Step, but you're not face-to-face yet. Build trust, ask the right questions and never be tempted to sell your recruiting opportunities on the phone. Otherwise, there's no reason for the prospect to see you.

Build trust by asking people if they're available to speak. If you have permission to talk, then depending on who initiated the phone call, ask questions to sell the appointment.

If you called, try asking some form of these questions:

Don't Give It Away
Don't ever tell your prospect too much about your recruiting opportunities when selling an appointment.

The most you should say about your offerings is you believe you can help the prospect. To learn more, the prospect will have to meet with you.

- *How familiar are you with the (branch of service)?*
- *What are some of your long-term career objectives?*
- *What do you think you need to do to reach those objectives?*
- *What's your biggest challenge to achieving those objectives?*
- *What steps have you taken to overcome those challenges?*
- *How open are you to discussing how the (branch of service) could help you reach some of your personal goals?*

If the prospect called you, then ask some form of these questions:

- *What prompted you to look into the (branch of service)?*
- *Where are you in the decision-making process?*

- *What factors will you consider to make your decision?*
- *Who else, other than you, of course, is involved in this decision?*
- *What kind of a time-frame do you have in mind?*
- *What have you seen or heard that's appealing to you about the (branch of service)?*

Once you have the answers, say something like: "*It sounds as if we can help you. We've helped lots of other people with similar objectives and challenges.*" Now, ask for the appointment. For example, "*Would Tuesday be good or is another day this week better?*"

The second reason why you might fail at gaining appointments is if you ask too few questions and do too much talking. Don't fall prey to this temptation. Avoid telling and stick to asking!

The third reason for failure is expecting the prospect not to grant you an appointment. And then, when he or she doesn't agree to see you, you aren't disappointed, because the outcome has met your expectations. What does that mean—that you don't expect to succeed? Change your expectations.

You must convince your prospect that the appointment will provide a benefit, so be sure to ask the right questions and provide strong reasons to see you.

Here's an example of what you could say: "*I recommend we get together and discuss how we might be of service to you. But let me guarantee you this; if it looks like the (branch of service) won't be a good fit for you, I won't hesitate to recommend someone else. Does that sound fair? Now, what is a good day to get together?*"

How to Ensure Your Appointments Will Never Cancel

Here are some things to say to increase the chances your prospect will be excited about making an appointment to see you:

- "We have some great solutions to those issues you described. Let's get together and I'll show you how we can help you."
- "I'm glad to hear you have gotten to the point where you'd like to solve some of the things we've talked about. I'm looking forward to showing you how we have helped others like you."
- It sounds as if we might be able to help. When can we get together?"

Do you recall the goal of prospecting? It's to get enough appointments to guarantee you'll be in front of a sufficient number of qualified prospects that will help you reach your accession goals. It's that simple. However, remember, there are three parts: positioning, prospecting and pre-call planning. We'll talk about the often-overlooked task of pre-call planning in the next chapter.

Checklist for Chapter 5

☐ The second part of the Investigate Step of the IMPACT Selling System is the physical activity of traditional prospecting.

☐ Nothing is more important to your success than the science and art of prospecting.

☐ The better job you do of finding and attracting qualified prospects, the higher your closing average will be.

☐ Suspects are people you know something about, but they may or may not be qualified prospects.

☐ A segment is a specific set of suspects, who may or may not qualify as prospects, and they fall within the general niche you recruit into. Your overall niche is the people who could join your branch of service.

☐ Your future success in recruiting is in direct proportion to the quality and breadth of your prospect file.

☐ The recruiter who asks enough of the right questions, of the right people, in the right places, will always have plenty of qualified prospects.

☐ What are the chances of earning the accession? Remember the ratios:
- 1:2 Currently doing business
  (Still in the military, active or reserve component)
- 1:4 Did business with, but not doing business now
  (Prior service, but not serving now)
- 1:14 Never have done business
  (Non-prior service prospects)

☐ To get referrals, your applicants have to be satisfied, and you have to ask for the referral.

☐ Use the 'Parthenon' approach for planning your prospecting activities.

☐ A Direct Value Statement positions you to deliver a free, 15 to 30 second commercial for your service branch. It should communicate the fundamental reason for both you and your organization's existence.

☐ The primary purpose of telephone prospecting is to get a face-to-face appointment. Build trust, ask some questions, but don't oversell your opportunities on the phone.

Chapter 6
Investigate (Part 3) – Pre-Call Planning

Investigate: To gather sufficient information about your zone, target markets and individual prospects within them to enable you to make the best possible presentation.

The third part of the Investigate Step of the IMPACT Selling System concerns the physical activity of pre-call planning for presentations.

If you're the recruiter who knows the most about your prospect and can turn that knowledge into solutions, you're far more likely to gain the accession than your competitors. By now you should have carefully positioned yourself in the ways your prospects picture you exactly as you want to be seen, and you've prospected diligently to get in front of the right people. Now you have to guarantee your appointments shine. Let's talk about how to do that.

Do Your Research

Recruiters, as a rule, are people of action. However, at this stage you'll need to slow down in order to speed up. What does that mean? You'll have to take the time to develop an in-depth, meaningful understanding of what you're getting into. You'll need to know as much as you can about each prospect, before you get to the appointment.

Here are some useful questions to ask yourself before the face-to-face recruiting interview:

- Who am I competing against?
- What are their unique advantages? Strengths? Weaknesses?
- What is the prospect's timetable for making a decision?
- What are the prospect's availability constraints?
- What outcomes or solutions does the prospect seek?
- What is the prospect's previous experience, if any, with the military?
- How receptive is he or she to new ideas?

In Recruiting, Knowledge Really is Power

Sergeant Taylor had consistently been one of the top-performing recruiters in her organization. In fact, she almost always did better in her territory than any of the military recruiters she competed against. She was well positioned with the students and educators in all the high schools. Taylor didn't bother to visit junior colleges, vocational-technical schools or proactively use other strategies to prospect, because she got so many referrals from the high school students and educators. In the back of her mind she knew she should do more prospecting, but she decided to worry about that later.

But this year, it's a different story. Three of the biggest high schools where she recruited successfully have dramatically restricted access for military recruiters. Furthermore, some of the other service branches she competes against are offering tangible features and benefits she can't match. Besides that, her office partner made the local news for the wrong reason – an inappropriate relationship with a student. Although her record is impeccable, the word is out that high school students should avoid recruiters from '*that*' service, and those same high school students are now visiting with recruiters from other branches, instead of Taylor.

How did Sergeant Taylor get 'outsold?' What did she fail to do... and what did her competitors do that she didn't do? And now, what does she have to do that she didn't have to do in the past, but should have been doing diligently?

The concept of researching prospects also extends to your existing applicants. How often do you communicate with them and ensure they are still motivated to remain in your delayed enlistment or delayed entry program? Do your prospects and applicants still feel they are going to get the most value from your recruiting opportunity? Are you "*defending the high ground,*" ensuring you're not vulnerable to attack and the eventual loss of your prospects and applicants to competitors?

Research is critical to making an effective, powerful presentation. It's as simple as this: the more you know in advance, the better you can make your presentation.

The 'intelligence' you gather must be translated into knowledge you can apply to your advantage when you get face-to-face with your prospect.

For example: How valuable would it be to have the answers to these questions before the interview?

1. Does this prospect have the authority to say *"Yes"*?
2. Against whom or what will I be competing?
3. What questions will this prospect likely ask me?
4. What is the single biggest problem I can help them solve?

Sources of Pre-Call Planning Information

Smart recruiters use every tool they have to learn as much as they can before getting in front of their prospect to make a presentation. Here are some places to look:

1. Internet search for any information about your prospect (check for any listings of activities or organizations they may be involved in, awards or recognition of any kind, Facebook, MySpace or LinkedIn pages, Twitter updates, Flickr or Photobucket uploads, blogs etc.).
2. High school and college yearbooks and newspapers
3. ASVAB rosters
4. Separation rosters
5. Trade journals, magazines or newspapers
6. Other recruiters
7. People who know the prospect through any sort of interaction with them

Needless to say, if you begin a face-to-face interview without some of this valuable information, you are at a disadvantage. However, if you enter the interview with this knowledge, do you think you would be better prepared?

Developing Internal Support

Smart recruiters understand how internal support can make or break their prospecting efforts, particularly in educational institutions. They also understand every organization will have two structures, formal and informal.

A Lesson from History

Napoleon: *"To be outmaneuvered? Yes. To be surprised? Never!"* Like Napoleon, good recruiters never allow themselves to be surprised by anything. Proper pre-call planning guarantees surprises are held to a minimum. For example, if you lose a prospect to another service or civilian opportunity because the competitor offers a better one, that's being outmaneuvered. However, if you had no idea your prospect was negotiating with another service or civilian opportunity while he or she was processing with you, that's being surprised. Don't be afraid to ask your prospect about other opportunities they might be pursuing, but do so in ways that are not critical or condescending.

The formal structure is the way an organization is supposed to work. For example, the principal is supposed to oversee the day to day activities and policies of a school. However, the informal is the way it really works. Perhaps there's a guidance counselor or faculty member you can develop a close working relationship with who is willing to represent your interests at the school. He or she may be able to persuade the principal to allow you greater access to the school's facilities.

Even though you may get greater support and accomplish more by working with the informal structure, be careful never to violate the formal structure. For example, if school policy says all visitors must sign in at the front office, do it. Don't think for a moment that because you get along great with a coach or counselor that you're immune from the rules. Make that mistake just once at some facilities, and the welcome mat could disappear.

Your Prospect's/Applicant's Internal Support Team

No matter your target markets or which program you're recruiting into, there are usually four key players you need to identify. They are your prospect's internal support team. Some of these people will have input. Others will have authority. Some can say *"No"*—others can say *"Yes"* or *"No."* Some perform dual roles, and in some cases the role doesn't exist.

Your job is to identify the four roles, understand how each has a part to play and then maximize your relationship with each person.

1. **Buffer.** The person whose role is to keep you away from the prospect/applicant, or at least at a safe distance. Often this is a parent, spouse, boyfriend, girlfriend, employer or school administrator.

2. **Prospect/Applicant.** The person you are trying to recruit. Even though the person may technically meet all the qualifications for enlistment or commissioning, he or she may or may not have the power to make the commitment decisions. Someone else, perhaps a parent, spouse or another person you've never met, could hold the 'real' authority. You must determine the level of power or authority they actually do possess.

3. **Decision-Maker.** The prospect/applicant may want very much to commit, but may not have the final say. The influence of a parent, spouse, friend or employer could position any of them as the ultimate decision-maker. Therefore, it's critical for you to ask each prospect or applicant some form of the following question: *"Is there anyone else, besides yourself, who may be involved with your decision to join the (branch of service)?"* If the answer is *"Yes,"* you have to find out who those people are and offer them the opportunity to meet with you as part of the recruiting process.

4. **Internal Advocate.** Early in the recruiting process, this role is the most important to you. You need strong internal support from someone (ideally several people) who can provide intelligence, guidance, outright advocacy and, if necessary, subtle pressure on your behalf. Interestingly enough, those fulfilling all of these roles can come from anywhere in the prospect's/applicant's circle of friends, co-workers and family.

Battle of the Prepared vs. the Ill-Prepared

Sergeant Hayes and Sergeant Thomas both recruit in the non-prior service markets.

Hayes understands that parents, boyfriends, girlfriends and teachers will all have an influence on his prospects' decisions about joining the military. Consequently, he always asks his prospects about family and friends and even offers to meet with these influencers during the recruiting process. He realizes that if he is open and honest with those people, he will have a greater opportunity to gain the support of the people his prospects turn to for advice, and therefore he has a much better chance of gaining an accession.

On the other hand, Thomas likes to encourage his prospects to make their own decisions about joining the military. He purposely avoids asking questions about the people who might influence his prospects, because he believes they only serve to slow down the recruiting process.

Who do you think has been more successful working the non-prior service market?

Reviewing Your Resources: A Checklist

To be fully-prepared for every appointment, you need every tool available to you if/when you need to use it. Here's a checklist you could adapt to your unique situation:

- ☐ Relevant documents (fact sheets, brochures, promotional materials, etc.)
- ☐ Your notes on the prospect/applicant/influencer
  - Phone number(s) and address
  - Background information on your contact
  - Directions to the appointment
- ☐ Previous military records, if prior service
- ☐ Double-check for appropriate dress
- ☐ Backup clothes (tie, hosiery, etc.)
- ☐ Pens, pencils
- ☐ Sales aids and tools
- ☐ Business cards
- ☐ Appointment calendar or personal digital tool
- ☐ Anything you promised to the prospect/applicant/influencer
- ☐ Notepad
- ☐ Breath spray and dental floss
- ☐ Calculator
- ☐ Testimonial letters
- ☐ List of satisfied people you recruited
- ☐ Necessary forms
- ☐ Various schedules (Military Enlistment Processing Station Testing and Physical Schedules, Basic Training and Technical Training School Dates, Drill Weekend Schedules, etc.)
- ☐ Laptop
- ☐ Power cords
- ☐ LCD projector
- ☐ Connector cables
- ☐ Other?

Confirming Your Appointment

Never assume someone will remember your appointment. Instead, do all in your power to ensure you have the best chance of a receptive hearing. Consider sending a handwritten note, friendly e-mail, phone call or text message to remind the other person about your meeting. Some might argue this will give the person you're supposed to meet a chance to cancel. However, wouldn't you rather give them an opportunity to reschedule the appointment than to waste your time traveling to or waiting on an appointment that doesn't happen? Years of experience indicate confirming appointments *is* a productive practice.

You're Only Fooling Yourself

Sergeant Harrelson loves the rush of being a recruiter. The more people he can talk to, the better he likes it. He's so good at this that he believes he can walk and talk his way through anything. And he usually does.

However, recently he's lost several qualified applicants to other military branches. Why? He stopped taking the time to discover who the members of his prospects' support system were, and he didn't make any efforts to develop internal advocates. He didn't bother to learn how his prospects made their decisions about joining the military. And because he was so busy, he often showed up late for appointments, didn't have the materials he needed and wasn't able to produce a list of satisfied accessions his prospects could talk with.

How would you like to be recruiting against Sergeant Harrelson? How do your competitors feel about recruiting against you?

Mentally Prepare

There are fine lines between enthusiasm and competence, spontaneity and memorization, and over-preparing and under-preparing. Like lots of things in life, success really lies in balance.

Successful recruiters understand the importance of the relationship between preparation and realistic expectations, as well as the role careful preparation plays in performance.

Getting yourself 100% mentally ready before your appointment helps ensure a successful presentation. What does that mean? You're either early or you're late. If you're not at your prospect's or influencer's location, or your office for that matter, at least 15-20 minutes early for an appointment, you're late!

Why is that? When you arrive early for an appointment, you have time to get yourself focused on the task at hand, become familiar with the environment, review your pre-call preparation checklist and visualize yourself being success-ful. Imagine how great you'll feel when your applicant says "*Yes*" to the recruit-ing opportunity. Picture the precise way you'll thank your applicant and promise to ensure they will receive the benefits you discussed. Also, picture how you'll savor the congratulations, the accolades and personal satisfaction you'll enjoy as a top recruiter.

Visualizing your success is a powerful tool. However, notice that we talked about visualizing your final success, not the process of gaining the accession. There's a big difference.

Imagine how you feel, act and enjoy the fruits of your efforts after you gain the commitment. Look at the end result, not the process. Running through your checklist of the actual mechanics of the sales process can give you the added competence you'll need. Visualizing your success will give you added confidence. Both of these – competence

Abraham Lincoln

Abraham Lincoln once said: "*Each day you get up and make a choice that it will be a good day or a bad day. And either way you'll be right.*"

What did he mean? Your expectations play a great role in how things will work out for you. Mental preparation can lead us to success or self-sabotage. How do you mentally prepare? What are your expectations?

and confidence – are necessary for your recruiting career.

Don't Be Like Sergeant Michaels

The best way to be prepared is to avoid being like Sergeant Michaels. On a recent school visit, everything went wrong. His driving directions were incorrect, and he left his office later than he expected.

When he arrived precisely at 10:00 AM (the exact time of his appointment), Michaels didn't realize he'd have to park 500 yards from the main entrance and then have to stop by the front office for a visitor's pass.

By the time he finally made it to the guidance counselor's office, he spent more time apologizing for his tardiness than discussing the opportunities he could provide to interested students. He looked disheveled and acted disorganized. In fact, he never got on track and rambled on incessantly until the counselor said she had to excuse herself to attend another meeting.

How mentally prepared was Sergeant Michaels?

Physically Prepare

The only way you can physically prepare for an appointment is by arriving early enough to get prepared. You can't afford to be out of breath, perspiring and rushing to get ready.

That's precisely why effective time management and personal organization skills are required to pull this off. But it's much bigger than that. Successful recruiting requires physical stamina, mental toughness and the ability to perform at a moment's notice.

If you haven't kept in shape, sprinting to your next appointment will leave you breathless, stressed-out and ill-prepared to perform. Furthermore, if you haven't checked and double-checked your briefcase for the materials you need for the meeting, you'll likely have a creeping doubt about whether or not you're all set for the appointment.

If you waited to the last minute to prepare, it may be too late. However, before every appointment make a point to go to the washroom and double-check your appearance. Is everything straight? Little things do make a difference: makeup, polished shoes, gig line, name tag and ribbons.

When an appointment is not in your office, take a physical inventory of your new surroundings. What do you see? Are there brochures from some of your competitors? Are there awards on the wall? How receptive is the buffer to having you there? Are there any other items in plain sight that tip you off about things you need to know?

Preparation: Positioning, Prospecting and Pre-Call Planning

Preparation is essential in any venture. In recruiting, it's often the difference between success and failure. That's one of the reasons why the Investigate Step is so large. Devote lots of time to positioning, prospecting and pre-call planning, and you can have a great recruiting career. Fail to do those necessary activities and you will be mediocre at best.

Checklist for Chapter 6

- ☐ The third part of the Investigate Step of the IMPACT Selling System is about the physical activity of pre-call planning for presentations.
- ☐ If you're the recruiter who knows the most about your prospect and can turn that knowledge into solutions, you're far more likely to gain the accession than your competitors.
- ☐ Researching prospects is critical to making an effective, powerful presentation. It's as simple as this: the more you know in advance, the better you can make your presentation.

☐ Good recruiters understand how internal support can make or break their prospecting efforts, particularly in educational institutions.

☐ No matter who is in your target markets or what program you're recruiting into, there are usually four key players you need to identify:
1. Buffer
2. Prospect/Applicant
3. Decision-maker
4. Internal advocate

☐ To be fully prepared for every appointment, you need every tool available to you if/when you need to use it.

☐ Confirming appointments IS a productive practice.

☐ To be ready for an appointment you need to arrive early and focus 100% on the task at hand.

☐ Preparation is essential in any venture. In recruiting, it's often the difference between success and failure.

Chapter 7
The Meet Step: Engaging Your Prospect Face-To-Face

Meet: To engage your prospect and turn a potential resister into an avid listener. To develop trust and rapport while displaying your sincere interest in the prospect.

Engaging Your Prospects

In the IMPACT Selling System, the Meet Step is the first phase of the face-to-face interaction between you and your prospect. Its real purpose is to set the sales process in motion.

The Meet Step is not about you dominating the conversation, interrupting the prospect or 'selling yourself.' Instead, several key things need to happen:

- Build trust
- Build rapport
- Measure your prospect's receptivity
- Allow your prospect to carry on an unsolicited conversation – if he or she chooses to do so

Research suggests you have only 19-34 seconds to establish your credibility and convince your prospects time spent with you will be valuable. What does that tell you about first impressions?

Here's another important lesson from our private sector research. When thousands of customers who had bought from salespeople were asked what they would have those salespeople do differently, the overwhelming response was *"Open the sale better."* Most people had no problem with how the salespeople made their product presentations, nor were they even concerned about being asked to buy. However, they often didn't like the way the salesperson first engaged them. Remember, we've already established that recruiters really are salespeople, and your prospects are the equivalent of customers. Do you think there are prospects with similar complaints about recruiters – people who wished the recruiter opened the sale differently?

How should you open your interviews? First, understand your purpose is NOT to get your prospect to like you; your goal is to get him or her to 'trust' you. And there's a huge difference.

Trust: Your prospect's level of belief that you, your organization and your recruiting opportunities are credible, and you will deliver on every promise or commitment.

Rapport: Matching the pace, tone, behavior and actions of the prospect so he or she is comfortable that both of you see the world in the same way.

To do this, you must enter the face-to-face sales interaction with the confidence the Investigate Step has given you. For example, when you are well positioned, the trust factor is higher to begin with. Why? Because prospects pay attention to people they believe have something important to say to them.

Additionally, when you adequately pre-call plan, you can focus your attention on your prospect, not yourself or your problems. Your prospects will notice the level of attention you pay to them, and the higher the level of attention, the greater the trust factor.

Trust vs. Like
Weak recruiters seek to be liked. They dump benefits. Smart recruiters seek to be trusted, and they sell value. There's a big difference.

It's All About First Impressions

Unfortunately, some prospects think meeting with a recruiter is an interruption from the important or enjoyable things they want to be doing. Unless, of course, they see you as vital to providing answers they seek, benefits they want or solutions they are looking for. Therefore, you must avoid coming across as an intruder, a flesh-peddler or timewaster.

Fail to position yourself strongly and some prospects will only agree to see you if they have nothing more important to do. And unless you can change these attitudes quickly, you'll never get anywhere with your prospects. That means you must first

Inspire High Expectations

Does your prospect believe you have something of value to say? Prospects will pay attention to a recruiter they believe has something important to say to them. You need to position yourself as that recruiter. When you do, your prospect's first impression of you will be a good one.

reduce the tension that exists between recruiters and prospects. And make no mistake about it; there will always be tension during a recruiting interview.

Eight Ways to Ease Your Inner Tension

If you're nervous about conducting a recruiting interview, here are eight ways to help calm the inner you. It's essential to reduce the tension you feel, because your inner stress will transmit from you to your prospect. Try feeding your mind with thoughts like these:

It All Starts With You

Prospects can read you like a book. They instantly sense your confidence, your attitude about being a recruiter, your belief in the branch of service you represent and your personal comfort level with them. It shows in your eyes, gestures, movements and tone of voice.

If you don't relax, they won't either. If you can't reduce the tension between the two of you, you'll never get to the required trust level. Yes, it all starts with you.

• My purpose is to help this person identify their biggest problems and provide answers and opportunities they need.
• I generate value for this person.
• I am a capable and confident recruiting professional.
• My branch of service and its recruiting opportunities promise a lot and deliver even more. My job is to help this prospect experience that value.
• What my organization offers has far greater value than the commitment we ask in return.
• I care a great deal for this prospect, and I will demonstrate that caring by carefully prescribing solutions to his or her biggest problems.
• Recruiting is an honorable profession that I am proud to represent.
• If my recruiting opportunities aren't a good solution for this prospect, I'm fully-prepared to end this interview.

These eight affirmations are powerful, proven ways to feel better about yourself, why you're there and why you're doing what you do. They will enhance your inner self and your level of confidence as you begin to feel less tension and a greater sense of comfort. When you start seeing yourself in that light, you'll be surprised at how much more warmly your prospects will welcome you.

Affirmation: A present-tense, first-person statement you repeat to yourself regularly. The more you say it, the more it finds its way into your subconscious. And your subconscious is the source of all you believe about yourself.

But a word of caution: Before you dismiss these ideas as silly or ineffective, give them a try. Whether you've been recruiting for ten days or ten years, they are as critical to your recruiting success as product knowledge or technical selling skills will ever be.

Maximizing Trust

Here's three things you can do to reduce the lack of trust that can exist when you first engage your prospect.

1. Eliminate potential tension-inducers before the appointment. We've talked a lot about this, but it's worth mentioning again. Make sure your uniform looks neat, you're punctual, you know enough about the prospect and you have everything you need to be fully confident.
2. Look for ways to help people relax. A quiet, confident manner and a warm smile go a long way toward lowering resistance and tension. Use them.
3. Be a good guest or host. When you're in someone's home or place of business you're on their turf; abide by their rules. For example, graciously accept any hospitality your hosts offer, such as a place to sit or some refreshments. Ask where you can hang your jacket. Place your briefcase on the floor, not on someone's desk, and ask permission to place a laptop on a table before you do so. When you're meeting in your office, greet your visitors warmly, invite them to sit and offer them something to drink.

Tension Inducer: Anything that can cause tension to increase in a recruiting situation.

Don't Dominate—Participate

Be especially careful not to dominate the conversation when first engaging your prospect. In fact, your efforts to appear friendly, talkative and behave like Sergeant Sunshine can sometimes prove to be more of a detriment than an advantage. Quite frankly, our private sector research shows that salespeople who dominate the conversation and offer too much unsolicited small talk are generally seen in a negative light by their prospects.

The Statement of Intention

Your goal is to allow your prospects to talk about things that are important and relevant to them. If a prospect wants to talk, let them. If they don't want to talk, move directly into 'sales talk' by telling them precisely what you'd like to accomplish and why, by using a statement of intention.

For example, you might say, "*I'd like to have a chance to meet you and ask you a few questions to see if we may have some opportunities that could be of value to you.*"

The Bonding Statement

This is a concept too few recruiters understand or use. Instead, they have usually been taught to say something like, "*I'm here to meet your needs.*" We said earlier that people don't always buy what they need; they will far more often buy what they want. So, why not tell them that you're going to help them get what they want? Here's a sample bonding statement, "*My goal is to help you get what you want. And we've discovered that if we do that things work out best for everyone, and that's how I'd like to work with you. Does that make sense?*"

Some recruiters question the choice of the word

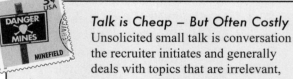

Talk is Cheap – But Often Costly
Unsolicited small talk is conversation the recruiter initiates and generally deals with topics that are irrelevant, uninteresting or boring to the prospect. Ironically, for decades, many military recruiters were taught to initiate small talk as a way of kicking off the interview. For example, recruiters were told to talk about subjects like sports, hobbies and the weather. Avoid those kinds of small talk; they add no value. But, does that mean all small talk is bad? No. If the prospect initiates the small talk, it's generally about issues he or she considers relevant, interesting, and exciting. Let the prospect talk for a few minutes before steering the conversation into sales talk.

"*want*." They say their primary job is to fill the needs of the service they represent. No one is denying that to be true; however, think of it another way. If you were car shopping and interested in one particular car, but the salesperson said you had to buy another model because it was in the best interests of the dealer to sell you a different car, you would probably walk off the lot, wouldn't you? It's an all-volunteer force, and your applicants have choices. You can't bully them into accepting career fields you need filled. Instead, you must convince them to fill critical openings by creating value for your service's features and benefits and showing them how they can fulfill their greatest 'wants' by accepting the opportunities you can offer.

The Soft Landing

If you really (and I mean really) want to build and sustain trust, an excellent assertion to make following your statement of intention is this: "*I promise you that if I can't help you, I can certainly recommend someone who can.*"

Think about that statement for a moment. You told the prospect you (a) just want to meet him or her, (b) would simply like to ask a few questions, (c) will determine if you can help, and (d) if you determine there is no way you can help, you will recommend someone else who might. This 'soft landing' approach will successfully reduce the tension level between you and your prospect.

Putting It All Together

Let's discuss the initial recruiting interaction. You arrived early or you cleared your desk, you have everything you will need, and you've invested time orienting yourself and mentally preparing for the meeting. Now, it's time to meet your prospect face-to-face.

"*Hello James and welcome… The purpose of our meeting today is to have a chance to meet you, ask you a few questions about your goals and dreams and see if the (branch of service) might offer some opportunities that could be of value to you.*

I can promise you this: if, together, we see that I can't help you, I will certainly recommend someone who I think can.

My goal is to help you get what you want. And we've discovered that if we do that things work out best for everyone. Does that sound reasonable?"

Some prospects won't say anything; they may simply nod. If your prospect remains quiet, move directly into the sales talk we've suggested.

However, most prospects will say something! They'll comment on the traffic, the weather, the appearance of your office, a mutual acquaintance, or even start asking you questions. That is 'solicited' small talk. But remember – the small talk must come from them, not you.

If they want to talk, here are some tips to make it more productive:

- Ask questions that get your prospects talking about things important to them. Nothing gets prospects involved in the selling process more quickly or effectively than inviting them to talk about themselves.
- Draw them out. As they talk, use follow-up questions. *"That's interesting, tell me more,"* or *"Could you expand on that?"* or *"What else happened?"*
- Listen closely. Visually respond to everything they say – nod, put your hand on your chin and lean forward. All these actions indicate you're interested and listening.
- Express genuine interest in what they tell you by feeding it back to them. For example, *"I'm sure that trying to work 40 hours per week and take three college courses at the same time has been challenging, hasn't it?"*
- Always remember the quickest way to get people involved with you is for you to get involved with them. What does that mean? If they're ready to move ahead, go with them. If they want to talk, talk. If they want to give you a tour of their house or office, take it. If they want to take you to the kitchen for coffee, go.

Sales Unscripted
Top recruiters don't memorize scripts. Instead, they speak in sentences that are comfortable and natural for them to say. We recommend you learn the basic components of the statement of intention and primary bonding statement and then modify the words so both these statements are yours and match your style of speech and level of comfort.

- Gain eye contact and lock into the prospect's emotions. Try to connect with what the person is feeling - about you being there, about other things going on in his or her life at the moment and about life in general.

One of the best ways to get people involved with what you want to happen is to sense what they are feeling. Put yourself in the prospect's shoes. Try to pick up on what he or she is experiencing in their life and imagine what it would be like to be talking to a recruiter about your future.

When you do that, two amazing things happen. First, you experience genuine empathy with what the person is feeling. Second, your empathy is transmitted through eye contact to the other person.

Some More Tips

Get to the point of your meeting quickly. Five things are uppermost in the prospect's mind from the moment you meet:

1. Who are you?
2. Whom or what do you represent?
3. What do you want?
4. What will I get out of this?
5. What's it going to cost me?

Avoid being abrupt. Novice recruiters may say things like: *"Well, I know you don't have all day to talk, and neither do I, so let's get down to business."* Or they may have been taught to ask a startling question. For example: *"If I could show you how to pay for college, you'd be interested, wouldn't you?"* In today's sophisticated recruiting environment, prospects will see that approach as manipulative and unworthy of their time.

Real pros take a more balanced approach. They ask non-threatening questions or make statements that gently open the door.

Make it natural. Let it flow logically from the rapport you've set in motion. Look for a tangible way to identify with the prospect and start from there. Search for a common interest, a point of personal pride or delight for the prospect, or a way to express concern over a problem he or she might be experiencing. Then, use that as a launching pad to shift into sales talk.

Discussions become more interesting to us when they become personal. Likewise, recruiters become very interesting to prospects when they become personal in a non-threatening way. But don't be artificial with it. False flattery, inane chatter and insincere comments create tension rather than reduce it. And we're not suggesting you fake an interest. If you are not genuinely interested in people, you'll have a tough time becoming a successful recruiter. But if you really are interested, just use a little creativity to find a way to express it.

By identifying with your prospects, you enable them to identify with you. You help to establish the feeling that you see life pretty much as they do and mean them no harm.

Building a Bridge

The shift from friendly conversation to active sales talk is one you simply must make, but when you make it, you want response – not reaction.

Perhaps the most helpful image that comes to mind is building a bridge across a chasm. The best way to move prospects from friendly chitchat to businesslike sales talk is to provide a structure to walk across.

The most crucial factor in building your bridge is knowing where you are and where you're going. One reason some recruiters fail is they start from the wrong place and/or try to get to the wrong place. They may begin with manipulative questions – the kind where the prospect can only answer "Yes" and then try to set up the prospect for the 'kill.' It just doesn't work. A better approach is to establish strong trust and good rapport and then convey value.

The bridge is one of the world's greatest inventions, and it's essential in a recruiting interview too. Bridges allow you to move from one stage of the sale to the next - in this case, from the Meet to the Probe. Building those bridges is easier when you remember to follow the three rules of IMPACT Selling introduced in Chapter 2. Again, here they are:

* Never skip a step to get to any other step. You started with the Investigate Step, moved to the Meet Step, and now you're preparing to go to the Probe Step.
* Make sure you and your prospect are in the same step at the same time. Invite your prospect to cross the bridge with you when both of you are ready for the journey.
* Don't leave a step until you have completed that step. Be sure your prospect is ready, willing and able to leave the Meet step and cross the bridge to the Probe step.

How to Cross the Bridge

To move from the Meet Step to the Probe Step, simply ask: "*To see if we can be of help to you, do you mind if I ask you a few questions?*" If your prospect says, "*No, I don't mind*" (which happens 99% of the time if you've been successful in

> ### Your Bridge Ticket
> When the prospect agrees to answer your questions, you've got your bridge ticket. You may now advance to the Probe Step. However, without permission to cross the bridge, you must stay on your side, in the Meet Step. Continue making every effort to build trust and rapport, and once you feel you've achieved that, try again to get that bridge ticket.

the Meet Step), you should then ask, *"Do you mind if I take a few notes so that I have something I can refer to?"* Again, 99% of the time your prospect will have no problem with that request either.

Why do we recommend asking these two questions? First, you need a transition to get to the Probe (*"Do you mind if I ask you a few questions?"*). Second, some prospects, particularly non-prior service ones, aren't comfortable with a recruiter taking notes or filling out papers during the early stages of an interview

(*"Do you mind if I take a few notes...?"*). This is a perfect time to introduce the Privacy Act Statement and assure the prospect that nothing the two of you discuss today will mean they are obligated to joining your branch of service.

Again, the Meet Step's purpose is to set the face-to-face sales process in motion while building trust and rapport. A firm base is necessary before moving to the Probe Step, where most of the selling really takes place.

> ### What Do I Do?
> If your prospect says, *"I don't want to answer your questions,"* what does that tell you? You failed to build trust, you didn't know it, and you moved to the Probe Step too quickly.
>
> If that happens, stay in the Meet Step and say something like *"I can understand that. You know, I was really intrigued by your earlier statement about your _____ (growing up in a military home, plans to attend college in the fall, etc.). Could you tell me more about that?"* Allow your prospect to continue talking, and don't be too hasty to cross the bridge until you're sure the prospect will follow!

Checklist for Chapter 7:

☐ The Meet Step is the first phase of the face-to-face interaction, and its real purpose is to set the sales process in motion.

☐ Several key things need to happen in the Meet Step:
1. Build trust
2. Build rapport
3. Measure your prospect's receptivity
4. Allow your prospect to carry on an unsolicited conversation, if he or she chooses to do so

☐ You have only a matter of seconds (19-34) to establish your credibility and convince your prospect that time spent with you will be valuable.

☐ Prospects will pay attention to a recruiter whom they believe has something important to say to them.

☐ Three specific things can reduce the lack of trust when you engage your prospect:
1. Eliminate potential tension-inducers before the appointment.
2. Look for ways to help your prospect relax.
3. Be a good guest or host.

☐ Don't dominate the conversation. Allow your prospects to talk about things important and relevant to them.

☐ Explain what you intend to accomplish during the meeting by issuing a Statement of Intention and Primary Bonding Statement.

☐ To cross the bridge from the Meet step to the Probe step, ask your prospect some form of these two questions: "*To see if we can help you, do you mind if I ask you a few questions?*" and "*Do you mind if I take a few notes so that I have something I can refer to?*"

☐ If you don't get permission to advance to the Probe Step, stay in the Meet Step until you build enough trust and rapport.

Chapter 8
The Probe Step: Asking Questions that Make the Sale

Probe: To have your applicant identify, feel, and verbalize their needs, desires and wishes; to determine what they will commit to, how they will commit, why they will commit, and under what conditions they will commit.

Here in the Probe Step, we are changing the term 'prospect' to 'applicant.' It really doesn't matter whether you continue to call the person you're interviewing a prospect or switch to applicant; your objective is the same. You are following a sales process with the ultimate goal of getting someone to commit to your recruiting opportunity. We switched to the word applicant because we believe that once you successfully transition from the Meet Step to the Probe Step you have established enough trust and rapport to believe the person you're interviewing is seriously considering joining the military.

The secret to successful recruiting – as we've mentioned several times so far – is to be in front of the right people, at the right time, with the right solutions, when they are ready to commit. What can ruin this scenario is the *"Fatal Flaw"* – to be so focused on what you want to have happen that you lose sight of what your applicant wants to have happen.

What do you think recruiters want to have happen? Gain an accession? Earn some referrals? Make goal? Win an award?

How about your applicants? What are they looking for? To have their questions answered? To be treated fairly? To have their problems or issues resolved? To satisfy certain needs? To enjoy the benefits offered to members of your branch of service?

If you fall prey to the fatal flaw, all of your positioning, prospecting, pre-call planning and meeting efforts will have been in vain.

Avoid the Fatal Flaw

Two errors can cause the fatal flaw to occur: poor listening skills and failing to ask the right questions. In other words, you might not be paying attention or you may lack the skill, knowledge, patience or know-how to ask the right questions.

Avoid the Fatal Flaw
Don't focus so much on what you want to have happen that you lose sight of what the applicant wants to have happen.

However, you can ask the right questions and still get nowhere, if you don't have good listening skills. For example, we could ask you what you'd like for dinner, when you'd like to eat, and even what you'd like for dessert and you'd give appropriate answers very easily. But if we fail to listen to your answers, the questions wouldn't matter, because we'd probably serve you the wrong meal at the wrong time with the wrong dessert. How about you? Have you ever been guilty of not listening to your applicants?

It All Starts With Listening

There is a big difference between hearing and listening. Hearing is the physical response of your ears as you pick up sound waves and translate them into signals you can understand. Listening is the active process of deciphering signals and translating them into meaning. It's the precise opposite of talking. Truthfully,

Listen Actively
Successful recruiters are good, active listeners. They are attentive to words, tones and gestures and can translate them into meanings. Without that skill, interviews become a *"monologue in duet"* or *"dual,"* even *"dueling monologues."* You will only pay attention to yourself and never recruit well.

most people are better talkers than listeners. They're much more adept at expressing their feelings and concerns than at listening to the feelings and concerns of others. How about you?

Tips for Being a Great Active Listener

Here are some proven tips:

1. **Open your mind and ears**. Switch off all negative thoughts and feelings about the applicant, and be receptive to the messages being conveyed.
2. **Listen from the first sentence**. Don't be thinking about what you're going to say next or planning the rest of your presentation. Put aside your agenda and give the applicant your undivided attention.
3. **Analyze what is being said and not being said.** Even the slowest listeners can think faster than the fastest talkers. Avoid trying to figure out what your applicant is going to say; you may miss what he or she actually says. Instead, use your faster thinking speed to analyze what your applicant is saying.
4. **Listen; don't talk**. Active listening is not only a great selling skill; it's also an important interpersonal skill. Always help your applicant convey his or her meanings accurately to you. For example, paraphrase what your applicant has said to be sure you understand when it's your turn to talk.
5. **Never interrupt, but always be interruptible!** Nothing cuts off the flow of meaningful dialog as effectively as continuous interruptions. What's more, it's offensive and rude. On the other hand, if you are talking and the applicant starts speaking, you should stop talking and focus your attention on what the applicant is saying.
6. **Ask clarifying questions that encourage your applicant to talk so you can better understand what he or she means**. Show that you're taking him or her seriously by drawing out elaborations and explanations.
7. **Remember what is said**. Log important points into your mental computer and on your notepad. Look for connections among apparently unrelated remarks.
8. **Block out interruptions and distractions**. Concentrate so fully on what's being said that you don't even notice visual and audible distractions.
9. **Be responsive**. Get your whole body into it. Look the person squarely in the eye, and use facial expressions and gestures to show you are listening to and understanding what's being said.
10. **Stay cool!** Don't overreact to highly-charged words and tones. Hear the person out and then respond.

Remember: your goal is to be an effective recruiter, not to merely *"get your two cents worth in."*

How to Discover What Your Applicant Will Commit To

Prepare the questions you'll ask. Unfortunately, too many recruiters think they can 'wing' an interview without any groundwork ahead of time – big mistake. Selecting a handful of broad-based questions and kicking off the interview with some of those questions will give your conversation a running start. Of course, every applicant is unique, and every situation requires some variation, but certain basic questions that come up in every interview should be planned in advance.

For example, asking *"What made you decide to contact me (or check out our website)?"* may provide you with the primary reason your applicant is expressing interest in joining your service branch. By carefully planning your questions, you

Three-Deep Questions

Every time you ask a question, be prepared to dig 'three-deep' to learn more about the applicant's situation, needs or problems. Simply stated, it means following up your primary questions with at least two more follow-up questions.

Here's an example:

Recruiter: *"What are your plans following high school graduation?"*
Applicant: *"I'm hoping to go to college."*
Recruiter: *"That's great. What type of college are you interesting in attending?"*
Applicant: *"A state-sponsored school with a good civil engineering program."*
Recruiter: *"That's interesting. What makes you say a state school versus a private university?"*
Applicant: *"I don't think I can afford the tuition at a private university."*

By going 'three-deep' the recruiter is able to uncover 'money for school' as a potential need. What could the recruiter ask about next? There are several choices. The recruiter could ask what steps the applicant has taken so far toward gathering the resources to pay for college. He can also ask the applicant about his interest in civil engineering and what he hopes to do with his college degree. If he did that, might he uncover a need for training and experience?

Always remember this key point when using three-deep questioning techniques. Every follow-up question should be based on what the applicant tells you when they answer your current question.

can cover all bases and ensure your wording is precise. However, be careful not to phrase your questions so they sound canned or come directly off of a government checklist.

Ask as many open-ended questions as possible. Closed questions calling for *"Yes"* or *"No"* answers discourage people from talking, provide only limited information and tend to set a negative tone. On the other hand, open-ended questions require applicants to tell you how they feel, what they want or what they think. There is room for *"Yes"* or *"No"* questions, but be careful not to use too many or to use them incorrectly.

Ask needs-based questions. You want to do more than get your applicant to talk; you want to find out what he or she needs. Therefore, frame your questions to allow your applicants to give you insights into how they perceive their needs.

Ask questions that help you identify problems to be solved. Usually there's one overriding problem that needs to be resolved in the applicant's mind – a situation you can pinpoint by asking the right questions. In fact, it's usually the primary reason why the applicant agreed to meet with you in the first place. Remember this question we posed earlier: *"What made you decide to contact me (or check out our website)?"* Plus, with proper pre-call planning and strong internal advocacy, you should already know what those problems are.

Ask questions that help you pinpoint the dominant buying motivations. Buying motivations and needs are not always the same. Buying motivations have to do with desires, feelings, tastes, and so on.

Avoid offensive questions or asking questions in an insensitive way. Certain types of questions can offend applicants and cause them to back away from you. Here are some examples of pitfalls to avoid:

- Don't use leading or *'setup'* questions such as, *"You can afford free training, can't you?"* What is the applicant going to say? *"No! I can't!"*
- Probe; don't pry. Nosey questions can be a real turnoff.
- Be careful about phrasing. For example, don't ask: *"Why would you even think about joining another branch of service?"* Phrase it more positively: *"What have you seen from other branches of service that appeals to you?"*

Ask questions that are easy to answer. Questions requiring knowledge applicants don't have can often make them feel stupid or embarrassed. For example, asking most applicants, *"What's the total cost of a four-year degree, including* *books, room, board, tuition, student fees and transportation at XYZ University?"* might get you a dumb look for an answer. The smarter you make your applicants feel, the smarter they'll think you are and the more they'll like you.

Use questions to guide the interview and keep the tone positive.
Some people love to ramble on and on, but by skillfully using questions, you can keep the interview focused and moving in the right direction.

Also, ask questions to which people can easily respond in a positive manner. Studies have shown that most people much prefer to agree than to assert themselves and disagree. Make it easy to say "*Yes.*"

Avoid These Three Pitfalls
There are three pitfalls to avoid when you ask questions:
1. Don't ask a question and then answer it for your applicant.
2. Don't interrupt your applicant when he or she is talking.
3. Don't fail to ask follow-up questions when you uncover a real issue you can help your applicant resolve with your recruiting opportunities. For example: "*Tell me more,*" then "*Could you expand on that?*" and finally, "*What was the result?*"

Ask – and then listen. Applicants can't talk while you're talking. Besides, you can't learn while you're talking. Don't just get quiet and think up something to say next; instead, listen to every word your applicants say and analyze the words, tones and gestures.

Remember: it's very difficult to talk applicants into committing; however, you can often listen your applicants into committing. Questions are your greatest selling tool, and the better you are at asking them, the easier it is to be successful.

We're sure you've heard the adage about how if you give someone a fish he or she eats for a day, but if you teach someone to fish, he or she will eat for a lifetime. Let's teach you how to fish for the right answers by showing you how to construct the right questions.

It's All About Solving Challenges

All things being equal, applicants will act fastest on a commitment decision to alleviate a problem, challenge, or difficulty they're facing with a current situation. Ideally, through your internal advocates or influencers and your pre-call planning activities, you should know what's driving your applicant's interest in joining your branch of service. If that's the case, prepare questions like these in advance:

- What are you looking for in a job or career opportunity that you haven't found so far? (Challenge: Satisfaction)
- What's the biggest obstacle you're facing with regard to completing your college education? (Challenge: Money)
- What technical skills do you need to qualify for the type of job you are looking for? (Challenge: Training)

Challenge Identification Questions

To develop these questions, simply list the single biggest challenge or set of challenges your applicant is facing, such as a lack of marketable job skills. Next, develop a question you can ask about that challenge, such as *"What type of training or education do you need to compete for the type of job you'd like to have?"* Now, develop three follow-up questions, such as *"What will happen if you don't get the training?"* *"How long could you put up with your current job?"* and *"What needs to be resolved to get you the training you need for a better job?"*

If you're not able to learn enough about your applicant before getting face-to-face, you may have to rely on more general questions like this: *"Many of the students from your high school whom I talk to say their biggest challenge about going to college is coming up with the money to pay for school. What has been your experience with this issue?"*

How Do Your Features and Benefits Stack Up?

Many recruiters believe their applicants agree to join based on features offered by their branch of service. Do yours? We'll bet they're more likely to join based on the benefits those features deliver. A feature is how an offering is described (i.e., Montgomery G. I. Bill). The benefit is what it will do for your applicant. (*"It'll offset the costs of your college education."*)

Benefit-driven questions help you determine if your applicant even needs or wants the features

Sell Benefits, Not Features

When you sell benefits, you're focusing on your applicants, their needs and what's of interest to them. When you sell features, you're focusing on the entitlements and various programs offered by your branch of service.

If a benefit of your recruiting opportunity is of no value to your applicant, he or she certainly does not need the feature, no matter what you think of it.

that drive the benefit. Here are some examples:

- What are your plans for higher education? (feature: educational assistance programs; benefit: money to pay for college)
- How much do you spend on groceries each month? (feature: commissary shopping; benefit: cheaper groceries)
- What sort of health insurance do you have? (feature: government-sponsored health insurance; benefit: free or less expensive health insurance to help protect you and your family)

But think about this for a minute. What if you already knew the answers to these questions *before* you ever got to this point? What if your internal advocate told you about the problems your applicant is having and the benefits he or she is seeking? Your questions could look like this.

- Knowing you want to attend a private university to become an engineer, how important is it for you to avoid having to take out large loans to pay for school?
- Understanding you have four children, how valuable is it for you to save money on groceries every time you shop?
- I understand your present job doesn't offer an employer-sponsored health insurance program. What steps have you taken to avoid having to pay high medical bills out of your own pocket?

Feature/Benefit Questions

To develop feature/benefit questions, write down every feature your branch of service offers, and then list the corresponding benefit next to each feature. To explain the benefit, simply ask yourself this question, *"What does this feature do for my applicant?"*

As an example, let's use the feature Servicemembers Group Life Insurance (SGLI). Ask yourself *"What does SGLI do for my applicant?"* Answer: *"It provides low-cost financial protection for the family of a servicemember who dies."*

Now, develop a question relative to the benefit. For example: *"How well would your family get along financially if you died?"*

Do this with every feature and benefit your service branch offers, and you'll have more questions than you'll ever need!

This scenario, by the way, will be the same for every type of question you'll ask. Here's the secret: the Investigate step will tell you every question to ask before you ever meet with your applicant! That's because most of the selling occurs in the Investigate and Probe Steps.

Needs-Based Questions

Fundamentally, your applicants are more likely to commit to joining when you offer them something they need, provided, of course, they really want it. Needs-based questions are the most basic questions you should learn how to ask. To master these questions, you must know the real needs your recruiting opportunities can satisfy. As simple as that sounds, it's not always easy. Recruiters sometimes become so focused on themselves, or the needs of the service they represent, that the applicant is never a part of the equation.

Needs-Based Questions

Get a pad and a pen and sit down somewhere quiet. List the features offered by your branch of service, and then, for each one, ask yourself *"What need(s) do we fill for our applicants with this feature of our recruiting opportunity?"* Don't be surprised if you get stuck at five or six features. But, trust us, there are at least 20.

Next, ask yourself this question, *"What would I have to ask an applicant to find out if each of the needs I've listed mattered to him or her?"*

Here are some examples:

Needs:	Question to ask:
Money for college	• How do you plan to pay for college?
Prestige	• What would becoming a commissioned officer mean to you?
Recreation	• What kind of physical fitness activities do you enjoy?

So, let me ask you a question. What needs do you fill for your applicants? Do you really know? Do they commit for financial or personal gain? To solve a problem? Sense of duty? Job satisfaction? To provide security for their family members? There are as many reasons as there are features of your recruiting opportunity. Let's use an example. Imagine for a moment that you recruit non-prior service enlisted applicants. Among other needs, these applicants likely require:

1. Job training
2. A fair salary
3. Affordable housing
4. Health care benefits
5. Job security

How would you discover these needs if you don't ask the right questions?

1. What type of career work would you like to do? What type of training or experience do you need to get the job you'd like to have?
2. How well are you doing at reaching your personal financial goals? Do you believe you're earning enough in your present job to live the lifestyle you'd like?
3. What percentage of your current income goes toward housing? Is your current housing adequate to meet your needs?
4. How would you rate your health insurance program? What does it cost you each month?
5. How often do you worry about being downsized by your present employer? What would happen to you and your family if you lost your job?

Objection-Based Questions

Contemporary recruiting is far different from old school recruiting where you'd have to memorize a whole series of canned ways to handle objections. The goal was to outwit and outmaneuver an applicant.

Today, your goal is different, easier and non-manipulative. You need to learn how to ask questions relating to the most common objections you'll get. Your applicant's answers will tell you one of two things: either you may not get the objections at all or you'll know exactly how to position your opportunities in the Apply Step to deal with the problem in a direct and honest way. Either way, you'll be far better off than if you didn't know the problem was coming.

These are among the three most common objections recruiters receive:

1. I want to think about it.
2. The commitment is too long.
3. I need to talk to my spouse/parents/boss or some other person.

And as frequent as these objections are, they usually come out of the blue for the unskilled recruiter.

The good news is there are some questions you can ask in the Probe Step to pre-empt these objections. Three potential applicant responses are listed after each question:

Objection 1: What type of process do you use for career decisions like this, and how far along are you on that process?
1. *"I'd like to think about it."*
2. *"I'd like to think about things but am prepared to make a decision within 10 days."*
3. *"I'm making a decision this week."*

Objection 2: What type of time frame do you have in mind for joining?
1. *"I'll need to check with my family to find that out."*
2. *"I haven't established a set date; I'm talking to other recruiters to get an idea about what they can offer me."*
3. *"I'd like to wait until after summer vacation."*

Objection 3: Who else, other than you, of course, will be involved in making this decision?
1. *"I need to talk to my parents."*
2. *"I'll be involved, but my spouse will make the final call."*
3. *"I'm making the decision myself."*

Do you notice how effective it is to ask the questions in the Probe step and how silly you will look later in the recruiting process if you don't ask the right questions now? In each case, by asking the right questions, no matter what the answer, you'll have somewhere to go with your sales strategy. If you do not ask the

Think Negatively
List the most common objections you hear and then develop a question or two that you could ask in the Probe step to tell you exactly how to handle each one most effectively.

Here are two examples:
Objection: The applicant needs to talk it over with their parents.
Probe question: Who else, besides yourself, is involved with your decision to join?
Objection: I'm concerned about deploying too often.
Probe question: How familiar are you with our deployment policies?

questions soon enough, you will face very difficult objections later.

Generic Questions

Most people like things to be easy, and that probably includes you, too. So, to accomplish that goal, let's examine some generic questions that have proven to be winners over the years for recruiters. You'll notice the questions are not numbered. That's because they're not designed to be asked in a specific order like questions on a government checklist. Nor do you need to, or should you, use every question in every interview.

We recommend you pick five to seven questions you like and have them on a sheet of paper in front of you. As you ask some of these questions, depending how the applicant answers, you'll be able to come up with more questions on your own to 'dig deeper' into the applicant's situation.

- What do you know about the (branch of service)?
- What do you know about the lifestyle of the (branch of service)?
- How flexible are you in terms of specific job categories?
- How important are long-term objectives to you?
- What are your long-term career objectives?
- How much flexibility is there in your current weekly schedule?
- What do you do on your weekends?
- What do you do in terms of hobbies?
- What do you do with your spare time?
- Why did you leave active duty?
- What did you like most about active duty?
- If you could change anything about your military experience, what would it be?
- What are the things you look for most in a job?
- What are the things that are absolutely unacceptable to you in any job?
- What's your availability to take the ASVAB and physical?
- What are some of the major changes in your lifestyle, if any, in the past six months?
- What impact have these had on your career plans?
- What, if anything, are you looking for in a job that you haven't found?
- What kind of time frame are you working within to make a change?
- What have you seen that's particularly appealed to you in career opportunities?
- What process do you use to make this type of decision?
- Who else, other than you, of course, is involved in this decision?

- What is it in your current situation that you absolutely do not want to change?
- If you could change anything about your current situation, what would it be?
- What is the single thing that's most important to you about this type of decision?
- If we were able to help you out, what would it mean to you?

Silver Bullet Questions

Think of these questions as silver bullets for your recruiting pistol. You'll notice these questions are similar to the generic questions, but contain blank spaces. You can fill in those spaces with words that fit each applicant's unique situation.
Feel free to copy these questions and use them over and over again. They'll serve you well no matter what service you represent or target market you recruit into.

- What are some of the major _____ within your _____ in the past _____ _____?
- What impact have these had on your _____?
- What, if anything, are you looking for _____ _____ _____ that you haven't found?
- What do you like most about _____?
- What kind of _____ _____ are you working within?
- What kind of _____ _____ do you have in mind?
- What have you seen that's particularly _____ to you?
- What _____ do you use to make this type of _____?
- _____ _____, other than you, of course, is involved in this decision?
- What is it in your current situation that you absolutely do not _____ _____ _____?
- If you could change _____ about your current situation, _____ _____ _____?
- What is the single thing that's most important to you about _____?
- If we were able to solve your problem what would this mean to _____ _____?
- What would it mean to you _____?

Prepare Completely Before You Continue

This secret is worth its weight in gold. Remember the IMPACT Selling System rule that says you should never go to a step until you have exhausted the previous step?

This rule is especially true in the Probe step. Here's why. Far too many recruiters will uncover one benefit the applicant shows some interest in receiving, one problem they can solve or one need they can fill and instantly the recruiter jumps ahead to the Apply step. A perfect example is the applicant who says he plans on going to college after high school. Immediately upon hearing the word 'college,' some recruiters stop asking questions and start '*telling*' the applicant all about the great programs their branch of

It's All in the Stars

Each time you ask a question and uncover a specific issue you can solve, place a star or asterisk next to the applicant's answer that you've written down. We strongly recommend you uncover a minimum of three stars – that's good. However, five stars are great, and if you find seven stars, you're almost certain to sell the applicant on joining. Follow these numbers and you'll be in a position to move on, but not until then. Don't give in to temptation to leave the Probe Step with only one or two stars or you'll be going forward with a half-empty gun!

service offers to offset tuition costs. Suddenly, educational benefits are the only things the recruiter talks about. They forget to ask questions that might uncover

Petty Officer Waymon and Sergeant Billings

Both recruiters work the non-prior service markets in the same town. At the end of the Probe Step, Petty Officer Waymon told his applicant, "*What I understood you to say is that you'd like to receive state-of-the art technical training, educational benefits that would allow you to attend college full-time after your service commitment is complete, and you'd like to travel to places you've never been to before. Is that correct?*"

His applicant's response: "*Yes, that's exactly correct. And I'd also like to talk to you about how I could possibly use some of the educational benefits while I'm on active duty.*"

Here's how Sergeant Billings handled the same applicant:
"*I can help you get a job you want, but let me tell you about the new bonuses we've got for some of the jobs my service wants me to fill. I can get you more money up front if you take one of these jobs; you'd have enough money from a bonus to put a down payment on a nice car. And if you're not planning on making the service a career it really doesn't make much difference what job you do for four years, does it? You'll get great college benefits either way.*"

Waymon summarized what he heard the applicant tell him, and it opens the door to meeting this person's needs. On the other hand Billings launched into a feature-selling spiel that may seem more in his best interest than his applicant's.

four or five more reasons why joining their branch of the military would be a great career opportunity. Don't make that mistake! Never go into a gunfight with a half-loaded gun. Uncover as many needs, problems, benefits, answers, solutions or issues you can solve as is humanly possible. Before you ever think about leaving the Probe Step, load your gun completely.

Remember that you've been recording your applicant's answers on your notepad or pre-prepared sheet of questions you developed. As you wrap-up the Probe Step, it's time to issue a summary statement. This is simply a reflective process where you clarify and sum up what your applicant has told you is important.

The Most powerful Word You Can Use

Professionals sell advice. The only way to give valuable advice is by asking the right questions and then making a strong recommendation. Therefore, the most powerful word you can use is 'recommend,' and it's easy to use it correctly.

Are You Missing Anything?

What if your applicant's answer is something like "*No, that's not what I meant. What I really want is ...*" No problem. Simply ask your applicant some form of this question: "*Is there anything else I missed?*" By asking a question, you're returning to the Probe Step to identify what you misunderstood or to discover if there's anything else the applicant wants to discuss. Once you're sure your applicant has explained his or her situation, issue a revised summary statement that captures the new information.

Issue a summary statement once you understand the opportunity or solution your applicant is looking for. For example: "*I understand you're looking for a way to finance your college education, to work for an organization where you feel like you're part of a team, and you want to believe the work you do is important and satisfying.*" Then determine if your understanding is accurate by asking, "*Is that correct?*" When you get a positive response, you simply say, "*Based on what you're after, I'm going to recommend _____.*" Fill in the blank with the solution you're recommending – the one that fits their requirements perfectly!

Depending upon where you are in the recruiting process, your recommendations must fit the applicant's situation or stage of processing. For example, during initial face-to-face interviews, the applicants may give indications they are leaning toward joining; however, there's no way to know for sure they are fully qualified to join unless they take and pass the ASVAB and a physical examination. Therefore, your first recommendation may be for the applicant to complete the ASVAB and a physical. Without knowing if they are fully-qualified, you can't accurately recommend career fields or a date to join. Suppose during your first meeting you sell an applicant on a specific job and then have to tell the person later that he or she is not qualified for that career field? How do you think the applicant will react?

In short, don't rush the recruiting process. Research in the private sector indicates 80% of all sales take place after the fifth contact you have with someone. It's no different in military recruiting. You will have many contacts with all your applicants before they ever take an enlistment or commissioning oath.

The Probe Step is the most critical part of the face-to-face interview. Therefore, we strongly recommend you invest most of your interviewing time here. Don't be tempted to leave the Probe Step too soon or to be premature in assuming you know exactly what, when, how and under what conditions your applicant will commit to joining. Proceed only when you are 100% sure the recommendation you'll make is the one they'll accept.

Checklist for Chapter 8

☐ Probe: To have the applicant identify, feel, and verbalize his or her needs, desires and wishes; to determine what he or she will commit to, how he or she will commit, why he or she will commit, and under what conditions he or she will commit.
☐ The fatal flaw in recruiting occurs when you focus on what you want to have happen rather than on what the applicant wants to have happen.
☐ Good listening skills are vital to your success as a recruiter.
☐ Prepare, in advance, the questions you will ask. Open-ended, easy-to-answer questions will provide the best answers. (Refer back to the Generic and Silver Bullet Questions.)
☐ All things being equal, applicants will act most quickly on a commitment decision to alleviate a problem, challenge, or difficulty they're facing with a current situation.
☐ A feature is how your offering is described technically. The benefit is what it'll do for your applicant.
☐ Ask benefit-driven questions to determine if your applicant even needs or wants the features that drive the benefit.
☐ Ask needs-based questions to determine which features of your recruiting opportunity the applicant is interested in receiving.

☐ Ask questions relating to the most common objections you'll get. You may not get the objections at all or the answers will indicate exactly how to position your opportunities in the Apply step to deal with the problem in a direct and honest way.

☐ Don't leave the Probe Step too early! Place stars or asterisks next to key problems or issues you can help your applicant solve. Gather a minimum of three stars, but gathering five to seven is much better. Never settle for only one or two stars before leaving the Probe Step.

☐ 'Recommend' is the most powerful word you can use.

☐ Don't rush the recruiting process. You will have multiple contacts with an applicant before they ever take an oath.

Chapter 9
The Apply Step: Making Your Recruiting Opportunities Solve Problems

Apply: To show your applicant precisely how your recruiting opportunity addresses their specific needs. To make the correct recommendation of the opportunity in such a way that the applicant sees, feels and experiences the application of the recruiting opportunity to fill his or her specific needs.

Application-Based Selling vs. Demonstration-Based Selling

There's a huge difference between simply presenting your recruiting opportunity to an applicant and carefully tailoring your recommendations to solve a specific problem, fill an exact want, satisfy a stated need, or provide a unique answer the applicant is seeking. In the final analysis, the only reason your applicant would join your branch of service is if he or she can see that what you offer is more valuable than simply doing nothing or doing business with one of your competitors – military or civilian.

Four Pointers That Guarantee Accessions

Here are four suggestions to guide you in the Apply Step.

Pointer 1: Choose Only the Most Appropriate Recommendation
As simple as it sounds, choosing the right recommendations for your applicant is

It's More Than Just The Picture

Sergeant Merriweather was a rookie recruiter, and her mission was recruiting non-prior service and prior service-enlisted applicants into her reserve component.

Her supervisor gave her a standard script to memorize. It was the same one he gave to every new recruiter for the past five years. Along with the script came instructions to follow it word for word. Armed with her memorized presentation, Merriweather went to work, but she didn't recruit a single person in three months. Then she changed her tactics. She started going "*off the script*" and presenting her opportunities based on the answers to the questions she asked. If money was an issue, she stressed bonus career fields, promotion opportunities and cost-savings benefits. If education was important, she addressed tuition assistance, loan repayments and the G.I. Bill. If deployments were an issue, she talked about volunteerism and re-employment rights for members of reserve components. If career fields were important, she asked her applicants what kind of work they like to do.

Her accessions suddenly skyrocketed. What was the difference?

a vital part of the Apply Step. Yet it is also one of the most troublesome, for two big reasons.

First, recruiters often skip over the Probe Step and go immediately into a 'benefits-dumping' demonstration. After all, they reason, there's no need to waste time. Applicants know what they want, and they can show other features and benefits later, right? Wrong!

A recruiter once confessed he learned a valuable lesson by losing an accession he could have gained. A prospect called and said he was interested in joining the recruiter's reserve component so he could keep the retirement benefits he gave up when he separated from active duty. The recruiter set up an appointment for later that afternoon.

He was so excited because his headquarters just announced an expanded list of career fields offering enlistment bonuses. Once the applicant arrived, the recruiter wasted no time telling the applicant about the bonuses and stressed that each of these career fields included state-of-the-art training that would allow the applicant to attend a technical training program for up to six months. The applicant promised to think over the opportunities.

Two days later, when the recruiter followed up with a phone call, the applicant said he decided to join another reserve component. When the recruiter asked why, the applicant said another recruiter offered him a career field with a lot shorter tech school which meant he wouldn't have to take much time off from his civilian job. The applicant said the bonus career fields sounded nice; however, getting extra money wasn't his primary desire. He wanted to preserve the benefits he earned on active duty and not interfere with the time and effort he needed to put toward his new civilian job. Ironically, the recruiter said he could have offered a similar opportunity, if only he had known. That's when the recruiter admitted it was his own fault for not asking the right questions.

Very often you get only one good shot to properly present your recruiting opportunity. Even if you get that second chance, anything you'll introduce is anticlimactic. The best way to be sure about your recommendations is to probe thoroughly until you are certain about your applicants' wants and needs.

Second, recruiters often present a wrong solution because they choose their recommendations based on their own interests, not on the applicant's desires. For example, we once knew of a recruiter who carried only an enlisted accession goal. He came across a prospect with a degree in aeronautical engineering who was interested in getting a commission. The recruiter received no goal, reward or recognition for accessing officers, so he told the applicant that if he enlisted first, he could then apply to become an officer. Not knowing any better, the applicant enlisted. While he was at basic training, school officials noted the applicant's education level and asked him why he didn't enter the service through the officer training program, especially since the parent service had a great need for engineers. The individual explained that his recruiter never offered him the opportunity, but instead told him he had to attend basic training first. School officials removed the young man from basic training, and within a few weeks he was entered into an officer training program. We can only imagine what he thought about the integrity of his recruiter or what he told his friends, especially when service policy was to place applicants into the highest program they are were eligible to be recruited into.

Contests Can Hurt

A problem with recruiting contests is they often encourage recruiters to show one program or career field to every applicant, because that's what their parent service needs and is pushing at the moment. As a consequence, you'll often walk out with no accession, rather than accessing that same applicant in another opening.

The right recommendation is always the one the applicant is most likely to commit to. Never forget, it's an all-volunteer force, and applicants have choices, particularly between military branches. If you try to overpower their wants with your needs, you're going to lose.

Pointer 2: Tailor the Presentation to the Applicant's Needs and Wants
When presenting your recruiting opportunity, you face four possible focal points:

1. You can focus on the benefits; this is what many recruiters do. Some recruiters love to talk about everything an applicant can receive by joining their branch of service.
2. You can focus on the branch of service you represent and talk about its mission and reputation. You might even make the mistake of telling your applicant the needs of your branch of service come first. Why is that a mistake? As we said before, it's an all-volunteer force, and your applicants have other choices. For example, suppose you were interested in buying a certain type of vehicle, and the car salesperson told you that you that the needs of his dealership came first. What if he said you would have to buy the car the dealership wanted to sell you instead of the one you wanted to own? Would you stay on the lot and only buy what the salesperson wants to sell you or would you go somewhere else?
3. You can focus attention on yourself by noting that if you surpass your goals you will receive recognition, an award or perhaps a promotion.
4. You can focus on the applicant – what he or she wants or needs and what he or she will gain by joining your branch of service.

Let us share a little secret: most applicants don't care about the first three, but if you hit on number four, you have a good chance of gaining an accession. If you want to add more 'sell' to your show and tell, get very personal with it.

Pointer 3: Give the Applicants a Show He or She Will Never Forget
The 'show' we're talking about here is not the face-to-face version of a carefully-scripted and rehearsed infomercial, nor is it a piece of sales improvisation theater. Canned demonstrations are like a straitjacket – they restrict your ability to tailor your presentation to the applicant's needs and desires. However, that doesn't mean you need to go to the opposite extreme and stumble through a completely spontaneous demonstration.

Actually, the application-based approach to presenting your recommendations calls for harder work than a canned presentation. It means you have to know everything about each feature and benefit in your lineup – and you have to know it so well you can present your opportunities with equal enthusiasm and force in any sequence. And that's a big order!

Pointer 4: Involve Your Applicant from the Word "Go"
A friend of ours decided to join one branch of the military, and he went to a

recruiter to discuss his options. Since the recruiter's office was located near a military facility, he was hoping to get a tour and talk to some of the military personnel.

"The recruiter acted as if I were a draftee," the young man recalled. *"Every time I tried to ask about visiting the base or talking to some of the military members, he kept saying he was the only person I needed to talk to, since I wasn't in the service yet, and the other people weren't recruiters."*

"Did you enlist anyway?" we asked.

"Yes, but I processed through another recruiter who treated me like I wanted to be treated," he explained.

Getting applicants involved in the selling process is a more powerful way to help them experience the transfer of ownership, rather than relying on a contractual agreement. You have a better chance of gaining an accession when you help the applicant feel like he or she is already enjoying the benefits of being in the military.

Top recruiters know their applicants must experience the feeling of what it's like to be in uniform, before they will take an enlistment or commissioning oath. Consequently, they usually offer their applicants a chance to visit a military facility or an opportunity to talk with people who are currently serving. There is tremendous value in taking your applicants to a military installation, when feasible. When applicants visit the types of organizations where they could be assigned, or see and touch the type of equipment they could be working on, they start to take mental ownership of the military lifestyle.

Get Your Applicants Involved

Do everything in your power to actively involve your applicants. Don't sit with a giant desk between the two of you; sit next to your applicants. Paint a picture that lets them mentally experience your recruiting opportunities. Have them compute salary figures, bonuses, monetary entitlements and educational benefits on a calculator. Take them to a firing range; tour an airplane, helicopter or ship; eat lunch at the base dining facility; walk through a base/post exchange or let them see the physical fitness facility. The more of the military lifestyle your applicants experience, the more they can see themselves living that lifestyle. Fearful applicants don't make commitments. Confused ones don't either. Remove fear and confusion with active involvement.

How to Apply the Four Principles Behind Application-Based Selling

There is a big difference between application-based selling and demonstration-based selling. Application-based selling allows you to create value, stack benefits, reduce perceived emotional costs, and make a presentation that is 100% on-target to address your applicant's most pressing needs or situation. Demonstration-based selling is inflexible and leads to nothing but commitment problems. Avoid it at all costs.

Application Principle 1: The transfer of ownership must occur in an applicant's mind before he or she will agree to commit.

The mental transfer of ownership can only occur when you actively involve your applicant and enable him or her to experience the lifestyle opportunities of your branch of service. Remember: recruiting is definitely a hands-on activity – especially when it comes to your applicant's hands.

Sergeant Sandusky the Medical Recruiter
Sergeant Sandusky, a successful medical recruiter, insists every physician applicant he tries to recruit has the opportunity to either visit a military medical facility or speak with one or more military doctors in the same medical specialty. What's the result? He has an exceptionally high closure rate! Plus he always seems to get plenty of referrals from the doctors he recruits.

Application Principle 2: All recruiting interviews degenerate into a struggle over commitment in the absence of a value interpreter.

What does this mean? Simply this; if your applicants constantly tell you they can get an equal or shorter commitment somewhere else, you have failed to create sufficient value for your branch of service. Your applicants are telling you they don't see enough benefits to offset the length of service they must commit to your branch. Consequently, the applicants have one single goal - to get a shorter commitment! More about that in a minute.

But first, what is value? It can be explained very easily, through the value formula shown in Figure 9-1.

Value equals perceived benefits over perceived price (commitment) and perceived emotional cost. Here's how it works. If your applicant believes the benefits he or she will receive by joining your branch of service are greater than what he or she will give up to get them (commitment) and any difficulties or concerns with processing, threat to safety and life, time away from family, length of training, loss of personal freedoms, etc.

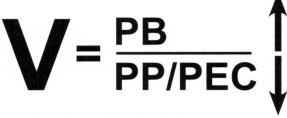

Figure 9-1. Formula for Value: Positive

(perceived emotional cost), your applicant sees value. When this occurs, you'll have no problem with the commitment length.

However, if the opposite occurs, you'll have problems. That looks like Figure 9-2.

In this case, your applicant feels the benefits he or she would receive are not sufficient to justify the price (commitment) and perceived emotional costs.

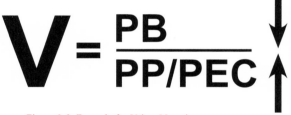

Figure 9-2. Formula for Value: Negative

How do you solve this challenge? Invest time in the Probe Step asking lots of questions relative to the benefits your applicant wants. Inquire about problems he or she wants to eliminate. Find out the needs he or she wants satisfied. Inquire about risks, problems, challenges and hassles he or she wants to avoid and issues that are important.

Here in the Apply Step you must address the benefits relative to perceived emotional costs. In private-sector selling, we teach, *"Never quote price to an unsold*

Perceived Emotional Costs: The amount of time, risk, change or commitment your applicants will have to invest if they join your branch of service.

Perception is important here, because to your applicants, perception is reality. You must create enough awareness of value to offset the perceived price (commitment) and perceived emotional costs of your offering.

Why Sergeant Rogers is Number One

Sergeant Rogers recruits officer candidates. He recently worked with an engineer named Tom and learned the following in the Probe Step:

- Tom desired a job where he could apply his college degree to immediate use. He also wanted to work for an organization that recognized top performers with advancement opportunities. And he also sought a position that allowed him to supervise, manage and lead people. Plus, Tom wanted to believe the work he did helped other people.
- Tom didn't want to start out at the bottom of the corporate ladder. Furthermore, he didn't care to work for a company where the only thing that mattered was how much money the organization made.

Here's how Rogers created value. He told Tom that before anyone becomes a commissioned officer in his branch of service, he or she has to have a college degree (benefit). He also explained the promotion system for officers, pointing out that it's designed to recognize and advance the top performers (benefit). Rogers also explained that officers are expected to supervise, manage and lead their subordinates (benefit). Next, Rogers pointed out to Tom that by joining the military he will experience the pride and satisfaction of serving his country (benefit).

Rogers then explained to Tom that he would be commissioned as a second lieutenant and how that would be the equivalent of starting a private sector career as a junior executive instead of entering at the bottom of the corporate ladder (emotional cost savings). Finally, Rogers stressed how the 'bottom line' in the military is not a dollar figure; instead, the real indicator of success is keeping the nation safe (emotional cost savings).

Had Rogers created value? Yes. Do you think he experienced a lot of resistance when he presented the commitment? No, and he gained the accession. By the way, Sergeant Rogers has been a highly-successful officer recruiter for many years. Are you surprised?

buyer." The same concept applies with military recruiting. Present the commitment only after you have created the right picture of value.

Application Principle 3: All military branches are similar until someone points out the differences.

Smart recruiters never assume anything. Just because your uniform is unlike the uniform of a recruiter from another branch of service doesn't mean your applicants understand the differences between the two of you. Many people think one branch of service is the same as another. Consequently, they may incorrectly assume the lifestyle and the benefits are the same in every branch.

Your job is to point out how your service is different and to do so without making derogatory comments about the other branches. Why? Because when you put down another branch, it reflects negatively on everyone in the military, and that includes you too.

Finally, never assume your applicant understands the benefits that the features of your recruiting opportunities offer. Always explain them.

How Petty Officer Edwards Ruined One School Program

Petty Officer Edwards recruited non-prior service enlisted applicants. He relied heavily on his school visitation program that included appointments arranged through the guidance counselor's office.

Unfortunately, Edwards had gotten a little sloppy lately. Although school policy required all visitors to sign in at the administration office, Edwards often neglected to get a visitor pass and started approaching students in the hallways as they moved between classes. One day, when a few of the students he was talking to were disciplined for being late for class, they blamed Edwards for causing their tardiness. The assistant principal called Edwards to discuss the incident and ask why he was walking around the school without a pass. Edwards accused the assistant principal of overreacting to the situation and said his military uniform should be the only credentials he needs. In response, the assistant principal advised Edwards he was no longer welcome on the campus.

How did Petty Officer Edwards lose this valuable school? What should he have done? What must he be sure to do at his other schools?

Application Principle 4: All benefits are intangible until someone makes them tangible; and all intangible benefits can be made tangible.

Think about the 'personal satisfaction' benefit you can offer your applicants. How attractive would serving be without showing pictures of people in your branch of service doing their mission? Simply discussing something is not enough. Applicants need to see tangible evidence of what your recruiting opportunities will offer. The real role of sales aids and tools is to help you tell your 'benefits story,' not to serve as a means for presenting your branch of service. And there's a big difference.

It's All About Organization

Smart recruiters assemble their briefcase and organize themselves so they can retrieve or easily locate the precise sales aid at the exact moment they need it.

You also need to know your collateral materials so well that if your applicant is keenly-interested in a specific feature of your recruiting opportunity, you're able to find the exact document, paragraph, or picture that describes or shows it. Amateurs either waste time pawing through their tools, can't find what they need or simply dump everything on the desk.

Four Proven Ways to Make a Better Presentation

Here are four tips for presenting your recommendations.

Tip 1: Avoid Making the Commitment an Issue

Interestingly, studies indicate the recruiter is often a lot more concerned about the commitment than the applicant.

Some recruiters seem to love to talk about the shortest commitment they can offer. They compare their service's recruiting opportunity with another branch on the basis of time an applicant must serve on active duty or the length of training schools. They talk incessantly about how 'quickly' the time in uniform will pass or how they'll be back home before their family has time to miss them.

Unfortunately, that approach only serves to remind applicants of how much the commitment is going to cost. Even when applicants are not overly concerned about commitment at the beginning of the recruiting interview, they become more and more attuned to it the more you talk about it.

Smart recruiters handle the commitment as a minor consideration. Of course, when the applicant makes it an issue, they deal with it effectively. But even then, they try to minimize its importance. The next three tips will show you how to diminish the commitment and perceived emotional cost factors.

Tip 2: Focus on Benefits, Not Features or Commitment

Do you recall the difference between features and benefits? A feature is an attribute of the recruiting opportunity and has some quality that makes it attractive. A benefit is an advantage a particular feature provides. Benefits are what an applicant derives from a particular feature.

For example, the commissary is a feature, and saving money on grocery shopping is the benefit. The G.I. Bill is a feature, and having money paid to you to offset the cost of school is a benefit. Space available travel on military planes is a feature, and the benefit is avoiding the high cost of an airline ticket.

The best way to answer your applicant's important questions is to focus attention on the benefits the person will gain from the features they are most interested in hearing about. This whole discussion may sound rather basic, but the difference in impact is enormous.

Think about this. All values are considered equal, until someone points out the difference! Smart recruiters never assume every applicant will automatically see how the G.I. Bill makes taking college courses less expensive. They show how much less expensive the cost of going to college can be by detailing how the program works.

Don't take for granted that an applicant understands the benefit a feature offers. For example, mentioning the Thrift Savings Program means nothing to an applicant if he or she doesn't know what it can do for them. Always point it out. The more benefits you apply to the applicant's needs or wants, the more often you affirm what he or she will gain by joining.

Tip 3: Focus on Value – and Then Work to Deliver It
Showing your applicant the benefits of becoming a member of your branch of service is the way you create value; in fact, it's the only way to create value. Furthermore, the more value you create, the more desirable the recruiting opportunity becomes to the applicant and the less important the commitment or perceived emotional costs become.

Nevertheless, go beyond simply verbalizing benefits and value. Work hard to make your applicant feel them. With a little ingenuity, you can usually get your applicant to express those values to you in his or her own words. Only then will you know for sure that your applicant has accepted the merits of the recruiting opportunity.

Tip 4: Relate Every Benefit to Value
Focus attention on value by relating it to every benefit.

The dictionary tells us that what gives an object its value is its 'desirability' to the person who values it. So your task is to translate every benefit of every feature into a tangible or intangible value – something the applicant desires. Create enough desirability and you've got yourself an accession.

What's the difference between 'tangible value and 'intangible value? You can see, hear, touch, taste, or smell a tangible value. On the other hand, an intangible value has more to do with emotions, logic or some unseen factor.

Tangible and Intangible Benefits

Sergeant Salter often speaks to high school seniors who are planning to attend college. He uses PowerPoint slides to demonstrate the various educational assistance programs offered to people who join his branch of service. His briefing contains a wealth of impressive charts and dollar figures to show the monetary value of taking advantage of these educational benefits.

Sergeant Hathaway likes to work with applicants who have families. She makes a point of building up the value of the military health insurance program by stressing how it creates peace of mind, minimizes risk and facilitates good health care. Which one of these recruiters stresses tangible benefits? Intangible benefits?

Could Sergeant Hathaway make her intangible benefits tangible? Could she show actual hospital bills and coverage the government has provided? Could Sergeant Salter show intangible benefits by pointing out how the educational benefits provide applicants the opportunity to grow intellectually and experience the satisfaction that goes along with advancing one's education?

How to Present Your Commitment and Get It

No issue nags recruiters more than this one. Exactly when and how do you present the commitment?

The 'when' is easy. Present it as late as possible in your recruiting interview. In fact, offer the commitment only after you're able to create perceived benefits that far exceed the commitment and perceived emotional costs. In other words, present it only after you have created sufficient value.

Your applicants are eagerly and appropriately interested in the commitment. And they should be. However, your goal is to avoid offering it prematurely. Instead, defer commitment discussions as long as you possibly can. Your aim should be to present your recommendations in a light that focuses primarily on the benefits to be gained instead of the commitment.

Applicants may ask you about the commitment before you've created sufficient value for it. Quite often, the commitment question will be raised in the Investigate or Meet Step. For example: "*If I were to join, how long would I have to stay in?*" You need to know how to deal with that question easily and quickly.

The best recruiters offer a response something like this:
"*I understand that commitment is important. And it should be. We've got a range of service commitments, depending upon your interests, qualifications, prior service experience, career field selection and some other factors. What I'd like to do is to make sure we offer you the opportunity that is exactly right for you. Then I can tell you the exact length of the commitment. Does that make sense?*"

This strategy of deferring the inevitable commitment question normally works well for several reasons. First, it shows you're listening. Second, it shows you're concerned about recommending the most effective solution for the applicant. Third, it communicates that you'll give the exact commitment. Finally, it gives the applicant a chance to allow you to go ahead without prematurely disclosing the commitment. And your applicants will allow you to proceed 99% of the time! On the other hand, if you respond to an early commitment question by saying "*Your military service obligation is eight years; that's four years active service and four years in the inactive reserve,*" what do you think the applicant will be focusing on for the remainder of the interview?

Commitment Pitfalls

When it does come time to present commitment, always offer it within the structure of benefits. Don't fall prey to the temptation to simply say, "*You've got to enlist for six years.*"

There are several other things to avoid when presenting the commitment. Let's talk about them.

Avoid Modifiers

Don't ever say things like "*Our regular commitment is…*" or "*Our standard enlistment contract length is…*" or "*The normal commitment length is…..*" Why not? Look at it from the applicant's point of view. If someone said to you, "*Our regular commitment is…,*" what do you expect to come next? Here it is: "*But for you, the commitment will be a lot shorter!*" Mention "*regular commitment,*" or "*standard contract*" or "*normal commitment*" and you'll be setting yourself up for that very same expectation. And when you don't meet that expectation, your applicant will either object to the commitment, ask for an exception to it, seek another option or simply reject the recruiting opportunity.

Avoid Setting Yourself Up For Failure

Common commitment presentation errors are statements like these: "*We really want you to join, so tell me what we need to do to get you to enlist.*" Or "*What do we have to offer you to get you to join?*"

That is not recruiting. It's begging. And you're not a beggar. You're a professional recruiter. Furthermore, when you ask 'begging' questions and the applicant

> ### Presenting the Commitment with Confidence
> Here's how Sergeant Steadman, an officer accessions recruiter, presented the commitment to one of his applicants who was selected to attend officer training, followed by a slot in pilot training. "*I'm thrilled to tell you the board results came back positive. Not only was your officer training program application selected, you also passed your flight physical and qualified for a pilot training slot. Therefore, let me explain everything that's going to take place for you. First, by attending officer training, you'll receive leadership training that not only applies to the military, it's time-tested training that works well in all walks of life, military and civilian. Upon graduation, you'll receive a commission from the President of the United States and the rank of second lieutenant. That's the equivalent of starting out your professional career as a junior executive. Your next step will be pilot training. That's approximately one year of the most advanced flight training in the world. You'll be instructed by some of America's finest military pilots and receive training valued at more than a million dollars. Then, once you've earned your wings, you'll fly one or more of the most sophisticated aircraft in operation today. Your commitment for all this education and training is ten years. Additionally, within two years of earning your commission, you'll likely be promoted to first lieutenant, and two years later, you can expect to pin on captain's bars. Furthermore, because you will be an aviator, you're income will be even higher since you'll qualify for flight pay. Finally, you once told me that every generation of your family has served in the military. You will now be continuing that tradition and experiencing the pride that goes along with wearing the uniform and serving your nation.*"
>
> Did you notice how Sergeant Steadman first reviewed the primary benefits his applicant will receive, in the appropriate order? Then, in the middle, he presented the commitment. He ended by adding in some more benefits his applicant was interested in receiving. The result? He 'stacked' the commitment between the benefits, significantly diminishing the perception of commitment and enhancing the perception of value. That's how to present commitment!

asks for something you can't offer, you weaken your opportunity even more.

Managing Commitment-Cutting Attempts

No matter how effectively you present the commitment, expect some applicants to seek a shorter contract, higher rank, different training opportunities, earlier or later reporting dates or additional benefits, such as a sign-on bonus.

Why is that? There are lots of reasons. For example, we all want the best deal. Also, there are competitors in the military recruiting environment with a variety of programs and incentives to encourage an applicant to join their branch of service. It's an all-volunteer military, making the recruiting markets highly-competitive and crowded.

Remember that your success in recruiting will be driven by two essential factors – conversion rates and volume. Smart

Never Compare an Apple to an Apple... Compare It to a Pear

Applicants will often want to "compare an apple to an apple." However, your task is to separate your offering from every competitor's offering so that it's impossible to make the same comparison. An apple is not a pear. Remember, almost every tangible benefit you offer can be matched or exceeded by your competition. Therefore, it's critical for you to focus on differences such as lifestyle, service mission, training programs, deployment policies and base of assignment options.

Never allow applicants to compare your recruiting opportunities feature by feature or benefit by benefit to any other competitive opportunity. When you compare apples to apples, you allow yourself and your branch of service to appear the same as every competitive opportunity – and you don't ever want to do that.

recruiters understand they are expected to fill the requirements of their branch of service. And they convince a high percentage of their applicants to join by presenting honest, exciting and appropriate recommendations, thereby creating value and reducing the perception of commitment.

It's All About the Math

To deal with commitment cutting attempts, or efforts by the applicant to "*modify*" the recruiting opportunity, try using addition, multiplication, or subtraction. Here's how that works. If your applicant says, "*The commitment is too long*" (a common objection), go ahead and acknowledge their response.

For example, you could say something like, *"To some people it does appear that way."* Then ask, *"What is it about the length that concerns you?"* The typical applicant response will be something like, *"It's the number of years I have to serve… it's too many. That's what I told you!"* However, your applicant might also have a different response like, *"Could you explain to me why I would have to stay so many years?"*

Now, you start to become a mathematician. Here are your options:

Repeat each of the benefits you can provide (addition):
"Let me tell you why our commitment is where it is."

Expand and repeat the benefits they'll receive (multiplication):
"Let me explain to you how each of the things we've discussed will help you achieve your personal goals."

Remove some features and benefits (subtraction):
"We can work to place you in a different career field (or in some cases a shorter enlistment). But to do that, you'll have to give up the enlistment bonus we discussed that goes with that career field (or length of enlistment). Is that what you'd like to do?"

Most likely, your applicant will not want to remove or reduce any benefits you've offered, and therefore, becomes more inclined to agree to your original proposal. The subtraction option is recommended as the tactic of last resort.

Another effective response to an objection about the length of an enlistment contract is to acknowledge the concern (as described above) and then add a statement about retention. For example: *"Six years does seem like a long time at first. However, in our unit (or service branch) our re-enlistment rates run as high as ____ percent. The fact is most people enjoy their military experience so much that they*

Addition: Listing each benefit you provide and how it helps the applicant achieve their goals.

Multiplication: Expanding and explaining the value your applicant will receive from each benefit you offer.

Subtraction: Offering to remove certain valuable components of your offer to reduce the perception of commitment to an acceptable level or to change the opportunity. This is your last option.

choose to stay even longer, many for an entire career."

It's All About Feedback

During the Apply step, you must be sure your applicant hears your message and your presentation is on target. Asking for the applicant's reactions and feelings does three very important things for you.

First, it lets you know where you stand. You might discover you can gain the commitment if you can clear up one or two issues. You might also discover there are several conditions to be met before you can wrap it up. Or you might discover you can't gain commitment under any conditions. At least you'll know what you need to do – even if it's to pack up and move on.

Secondly, you enable applicants to admit to themselves how they feel and give you an indication of how they'll act. By verbalizing their feelings, they often clarify things for themselves. You'll probably have smoother sailing once your applicants hear their own voices saying, "*I like it!*"

Third, it enables you to reinforce positive feelings and clear up any misconceptions your applicants may have. By getting their reactions, you will see if you communicated the message you intended to deliver. If they understand what you've said and feel positive about it, you can reinforce the values you created and help them move toward psychological ownership. On the other hand, you might discover they misunderstood some point you made. If so, you can clear it up before moving on.

Some Sample Feedback Questions

Have you ever had a conversation with someone who never asked you your reactions, level of understanding, or degree of agreement to what he or she was saying? Don't make that mistake when presenting your recruiting opportunity. Here are some ways to get feedback and determine exactly how the applicant is hearing, understanding and agreeing with your presentation.

- How does this look?
- Does this make sense?
- Does this look like something that could work for you?
- How are we doing so far?
- What do you think?
- Do you feel this could help you?

Where Do You Go?

To determine if your presentation is on target, solicit your applicants' reactions to what they see, hear, and understand. Their answers will provide a clear picture of how you're doing.

If you get responses like, "*I don't understand what you said*," or "*I don't agree with that*," don't panic. Simply ask what he or she doesn't understand or doesn't agree with, and be sure there's no other problems ("*Is there anything else you are not clear about?*" or "*Is there anything else you don't agree with?*"). Now simply rephrase what your applicants didn't understand into words they can comprehend or restate your position on the issue(s) they disagreed with.

- Do you understand everything so far?
- Does this look like the type of opportunity you've been looking for?
- Are we on target?

Checklist for Chapter 9

☐ Apply: To show your applicant precisely how your recruiting opportunity addresses their specific needs. To make the correct recommendation of the opportunity in such a way that the applicant sees, feels and experiences the application of the recruiting opportunity to solve his or her problem or fill his or her specific need.

☐ There's a big difference between simply presenting your features and carefully recommending your opportunities as something your applicant needs and wants.

☐ Four actions to guarantee success:
  1. Choose only the most appropriate recommendations.
  2. Tailor the presentation to your applicant's needs and wants.
  3. Give a show your applicant will never forget.
  4. Involve your applicant from the word "*Go.*"

☐ Four principles behind application-based selling:
  1. The transfer of ownership must occur in an applicant's mind before he or she will agree to commit!
  2. All recruiting interviews degenerate into a struggle over commitment in the absence of a value interpreter.
  3. All branches of the military are similar until someone points out the differences.
  4. All benefits are intangible until someone makes them tangible – and all intangible benefits can be made tangible.

☐ Value equals the perceived benefit over the perceived price and perceived emotional costs.

☐ To make a better presentation:
   1. Avoid making the commitment an issue.
   2. Focus on benefits, not features or commitment.
   3. Focus on value – and then work to deliver it.
   4. Relate every benefit to value.

☐ Avoid placing modifiers on the commitment length.

☐ Expect applicants to question the commitment length. Acknowledge and justify.

☐ Separate your offerings by comparing 'apples to pears.'

☐ Use feedback questions to ensure your recommendations are on target.

Chapter 10
The Convince Step: Making Your Applicants Believe

When people believe in something enough, they'll take action on it. Applicants expect recruiters to make claims for their recruiting opportunities. However, they are truly impressed when someone else makes similar assertions... and when they have the opportunity to experience the claims and enjoy the benefits promised to them. Before agreeing to commit, applicants must believe what they hear and feel about the recruiting opportunity.

Military Recruiting Is a Worthy Profession

Regrettably, there are a few military recruiters whose lack of credibility or integrity places lots of other recruiters in a bad light. However, you don't need to apologize for those people. Nor should you feel as though you should find another profession. Military recruiters are vital to the defense of our nation. Instead, recognize the negative perception that is sometimes held toward recruiters, and do something about it to ensure that same perception doesn't cost you any accessions.

That's precisely why the Convince Step is so critical and must never be short-changed, skipped or forgotten. Doing so sets you up for failure and disappointment. And yet, the Convince Step is often the most overlooked stage of the sale. Why? Because some recruiters feel it's not necessary, if the applicant says "*Everything looks great.*"

Unfortunately, when you don't exhaust the Convince Step, you open the door for 'buyer's remorse' to step in. On the other hand, a well-executed Convince Step will further solidify your applicant's decision to commit.

When People Believe Enough, They Act

It's not unusual to read polls show-ing varying degrees of mistrust about military recruiters. Occasionally, news stories will appear citing awful examples of recruiter malpractice. And while the majority of military

Integrity: Ensuring whatever you say, believe, or commit to do will be consistent with your highest internal beliefs and the core values of the military service you represent.

recruiters maintain their integrity, it only takes a few unscrupulous ones to hurt the reputation of everyone wearing a military recruiter badge. In fact, there's an old joke:

"Do you know how you can always tell when a recruiter is lying?"
"No."
"If he waves both arms in the air, he may be telling you the truth. If he jumps all over the place and won't look you in the eye, he still may be telling you the truth. But if he ever opens his mouth, he's lying!"

Just how deserved the reputation for dishonesty among recruiters may be is a matter of opinion. Valid or not, you cannot ignore the perceptions of the ap-plicants and influencers with whom you interact, because much of your success depends on people believing what you say.

A second important reality is that each applicant has his or her own belief system against which all other beliefs are measured. And, never forget, applicants will do what they believe is best for them.

The challenges you face can be stated as principles:

Convince Principle 1: When people believe strongly enough, they act!

If people believe strongly enough that what you are offering will be worth more to them than the commitment you're asking for it, they'll join, and if they don't believe it, they won't! It's that simple.

Moreover, if you are going to be successful, you must find ways to cut through the mistrust to convince your applicants what you say is true, and the benefits you offer outweigh the commitment.

That's a big order, but thousands of recruiters do it every day, and you can too. Let's explore how to *consistently* convince applicants of the value of your recommendations. There are four actions you can take to set the stage for your applicants to commit:

1. You can prove your claims.
2. You can bring your own witnesses.
3. You can justify the commitment.
4. You can relieve the applicants' fears of committing.

Let's examine them one at a time.

Prove Your Claims

It might damage your ego, but it will certainly help your production numbers to assume most applicants will not believe anything you say, unless you prove it to them. In all fairness, your applicants have a right to be skeptical about your claims for several reasons.

First, you stand to gain something if they believe you. Former Secretary of State Henry Kissinger told a story about a reaction he once got from the late Chairman Mao Tse-tung of China:

"What do you want from us?" Mao asked bluntly.
"We don't want anything but your friendship," Kissinger replied.
"If you want nothing, you shouldn't be here; and if I wanted nothing, I wouldn't have invited you here, so let's get down to business," said the crafty old chairman.

Today's alert applicants feel the same way. They know you stand to gain something if they commit, so they'll balance everything you say against that fact.

Second, they've been lied to before. Even though all military branches mandate their recruiters to follow policies, instructions and regulations to the letter, some recruiters stretch the truth enough that it essentially becomes a lie. Fortunately, when they are caught, they are usually punished and removed from recruiting duty. However, it may be too late for the misled applicant.

Third, people have become jaded by oversell. By the time the average person reaches adulthood, he or she will have seen more than a million television commercials and heard nearly as many radio spots promising everything from robust health and instant wealth to perpetual happiness. To survive, most people have developed very effective mental tune-out devices that filter out any promise they question.

These and other factors make the Convince Step absolutely crucial. You have to prove every claim you make about your offerings, your branch of service and yourself.

Here are some ways you can do it.

Claim Prover 1: Never Make a Claim You Can't Back Up with Facts

Personal and professional integrity are essential in today's recruiting marketplace. Honesty is vital -- making even one false claim will cost you more accessions than it will gain for you.

But there's another equally important issue. It's not enough for you to believe a claim is true; you must back it up with proof your applicant will accept.

Let's look at a second principle that can enhance your credibility:

Convince Principle 2: It makes little difference what you believe is true, unless you can prove it to your applicant.

It's as simple as this: one claim proved is worth 100 claims only made, and one false claim discovered can do more damage than a truckload of claims proved.

Never Presume Anything!

Can you remember the experiences you had with your recruiter when you joined the military? Looking back, did he or she ever misrepresent something to you? What did people say to you the first time you told them you were becoming a recruiter? Has someone ever told you about a situation where a recruiter misrepresented something?

How did you feel? How did your friend or family member feel? What is your opinion of the recruiter who was less than honest? Do you think some of your applicants might have had a similar experience with another recruiter? If so, do you think they may lump you in with recruiters who are less than honorable?

Never presume anything! Instead, take the approach that your applicants won't believe anything you say unless it's verified by something you can show them, do for them or they can experience to prove the validity of your claims.

Claim Prover 2: If You Can Prove It, Show Your Evidence

It's important to back up every claim you make, especially those that sound too good to be true.

The smart recruiter offers supporting data, relevant documents and tangible evidence to prove every claim he or she makes. And, since you can never really know which applicants will doubt which claims, the safest route is to prove them all.

> ### It's Too Good To Be True
> The more dramatic and outstanding the claim, the more proof it usually requires. If you declare to an applicant that by attending basic training and a technical training school he or she will earn 15 college credits, you'd better plan to show the evidence to back it up.
>
> Second, constantly make sure you give enough evidence for each claim. Always err on the side of caution and keep as much testimonial evidence as possible within easy reach.

Claim Prover 3: Reinforce All Claims Visually

"*A picture is worth a thousand words*" is an ancient truth. Most people believe that statement because it has proven true in their own life experiences. As a recruiter, it means your applicants more easily believe and remember what you show them rather than what you only *tell* them.

Simple graphic, illustrative and pictorial examples speed up your proof, make your claims easier to grasp and believe, and they also help your applicants to remember them longer.

Claim Prover 4: Let Applicants Experience It Themselves

"*The proof of the pudding is in the eating*" is a time-proven adage. If you claim the food is good in your dining halls, let your applicant enjoy a meal in one of your facilities. If you claim the gymnasiums

> ### Try It, You'll Like It!
> This can be a tough assignment if your office is not located near one of your service's installations. However, arranging a tour of a base/post where your applicants can witness the military lifestyle and talk to people like themselves who made the decision to join will strengthen your credibility and reduce some fear of committing.

on your bases/posts have great physical fitness equipment, let your applicants see for themselves.

Claim Prover 5: Repeat Important Claims and Proofs Again and Again

Have you ever wondered why major companies repeat the *same* commercials over and over? A company may spend more money on air time to run just one commercial than it spends on producing the product being advertised.

The reason companies keep running the same commercials is studies show it's the best way to get people to believe them, remember them and act upon them. When you're selling an applicant on your recruiting opportunity, the more often you repeat something, the better your chances the applicant will accept and re-member it.

Here's the second big task you have in the Convince Step.

Bring Your Own Witnesses

What do the courts view as the strongest evidence in a trial? You guessed it – an eyewitness! What is the strongest theme in advertising? Word of mouth! Like-wise, what's the most convincing evidence you can use to prove your claims? It's an endorsement from a satisfied accession!

The following principle explains why endorsements are so powerful.

Convince Principle 3: Applicants expect recruiters to make claims for what they offer, but they are most impressed when someone else makes or endorses those claims.

Therefore, never make a claim for yourself or your branch of service that you can get someone else to make for you. Now, let's explain how you can bring your own witnesses to boost your recruiting efforts.

Witness Pointer 1: Try to Get a Written Endorsement from Every Satisfied Accession

The best way to get endorsements is to ask for them. It's that simple! Yet you'd be surprised at how many recruiters either neglect it or are afraid to do it.

Explain to your accessions that since they have joined the same branch of service as you, you would appreciate an opportunity to mention them as satisfied applicants. Don't be surprised if some of these people volunteer to write a letter for you. If they agree to using their name but don't volunteer to write a letter, come right out and ask for one. From our experience, most people feel flattered to learn a letter from them will matter that much. Only a very few will turn you down, usually for personal reasons. And that reason could be that the applicant saw value in the overall recruiting opportunity, but may not have enjoyed working with you. In other words, they joined in spite of you.

To ensure you get the letter, provide the applicant with a self-addressed, pre-stamped envelope or suggest coming by a few days later to pick it up and save the applicant the trouble of mailing it. When you receive the letter, contact the person and say *"Thank you."* Interestingly, you'll be surprised at how many referrals you'll pick up on those second trips around.

The Sales Machine

The training branch at one recruiting headquarters got their recruiters ahead of the game when it came to testimonials. They asked every recruiter to send them copies of the letters they received from satisfied accessions. With hundreds of recruiters, that translated to a ton of letters!

But they didn't stop there. They posted the best letters on the organization's intranet, in different categories, so every recruiter in the organization could retrieve them easily. Now, regardless of which program a recruiter recruits for or which career field they recommend to an applicant, the production recruiters have a wide range of testimonial letters to choose from.

Could you do the same thing? It's just a matter of your initiative.

Witness Pointer 2: Carefully Select the Endorsements You Use With Each Applicant

Let's face it: we're all imitators. We try to be like the people we respect and admire and sometimes those we wish to impress. It's one of the strongest buying motivations.

Car dealers made an interesting discovery by asking people a few questions when they purchased a new car. One of the most frequent reasons people give for buying a new car goes something like this: *"My neighbor (or co-worker or friend) bought a new car, and I started thinking maybe it was time I looked into it."*

Haven't you tried out a new restaurant, store or product because friends said they liked it? Absolutely; we've all done the same thing.

The more recognizable a name is, the more convincing it will be to your applicant. That's one good reason to find out in the Investigate and Probe steps all you can about every prospect you meet. If you can produce an endorsement from a fellow student, business associate or personal friend of the applicant, it strengthens your positioning.

If you can't find an endorsement from someone the applicant knows, choose endorsements from accessions of similar ages, with similar interests and from similar backgrounds.

Witness Pointer 3: Treat Endorsements with Dignity and Respect

An endorsement letter is worth many times its weight in gold, so treat it well. That suggests several things:

First, always speak of your applicants and accessions as if you think they are the greatest people in the world. They are!

Second, keep your endorsements looking new by storing them in plastic sleeves inside a binder. Furthermore, keep the binder in plain site on a table in the waiting area of your office, not on a shelf. Visitors will glance through a binder on a table, but they won't pull one out of a cabinet. When applicants arrive early for their appointments and have to wait, you want them to read the letters.

Third, show your endorsements as if you are granting the applicant a special privilege to see them. If, for example, you rapidly flip them across a table at an applicant, you create several problems:

1. You don't give your applicant time to read them, so it appears you are hiding something.
2. Your behavior is contemptuous of both the applicant and the people who gave you their endorsements.
3. You make the applicant hesitant to give you an endorsement. Who wants to be included in an arsenal of missiles you toss across tables at people?

People who provide endorsements show a great deal of trust in you, and applicants watch the respect you give to the people you've already recruited. Therefore, treat them well.

Witness Pointer 4: Try to Involve Happy Applicants or Accessions with Your New Applicants

Sometimes you can get one of your accessions or an existing applicant to make an appointment for you with a friend, neighbor, or associate. If so, it's a convincing piece of evidence.

Consider taking both people to lunch together or meeting at a place other than your office. Ask your satisfied applicant or accession some questions about how things are going with their military experience so far. Watch the interest level of the other person build as your 'witness' says good things. One key point – make sure your witness is happy. You sure don't need someone saying they wished they'd never heard of you.

Justify the Commitment

We discussed justifying the commitment as part of the Apply Step. To repeat some good advice, "*When presenting the commitment, always present it within the structure of the benefits you are offering.*" In other words, justify the commitment before you even mention it.

Then, when you state the commitment, 'stack' it between the benefits and the perceived emotional costs, so your applicant understands the commitment within the proper context.

If he or she questions the cost of committing by making comparisons to competing opportunities, try the 'apples and pears' strategy mentioned in Chapter 9. If you present your offering as distinct from any other opportunity on the market, you make it difficult, or even impossible, for an applicant to force you into defending the commitment.

Relieve Your Applicant's Fear of Committing

Fear can be one of the strongest motivations an applicant may have for joining your branch of service. For example, an applicant may fear losing the opportunities you are offering, if they recognize those opportunities could help them achieve their goals. However, fear can also be one of the greatest deterrents to an applicant deciding to commit.

In fact, fear of committing often proves to be one of the toughest challenges a recruiter faces. It may grow out of fear of making a mistake, fear of ridicule or rejection, fear of the unknown, and the fears of being deployed, injured or killed. Your task is to help applicants overcome enough of whatever fear they feel to make them comfortable enough to commit. How can you do that?

First, we'll look at an important principle of convincing your applicant and then explore some techniques you can use to make it work for you.

Convince Principle 4: As trust in you and confidence in the value of your offer rises, fear of committing disappears.

The greatest fear busters are trust and value, and there are three ways to make them work for you.

Buying Fear Reliever 1: Reconcile the Commitment Decision with Their Value System

Any time we set out to act in a manner that is inconsistent with the way we see ourselves, we can expect to feel some fear. That's true even if what we are doing is a good thing.

For example, many people who leave a 'secure' job with a steady income to return to school and start a whole new career are scared they will fail and be humiliated. Years from now, they may look back on it as one of the greatest steps they ever took, but for the moment it is threatening to their value system.

That same dynamic often shows up when a person starts to buy something – especially if it costs a lot or it represents a significant change in their lives.

Persons who 'come and go' as they please, for example, may feel as if they are giving up all their personal freedoms if they join the military. The decision to commit may in fact offer tremendous long-term advantages for them, but it will feel like a violation of the values they have lived by for so long.

One of the real services you can render is to help them reconcile their choice with their value system. Thus, it is often helpful to openly explore the fears they are feeling so they can become aware of their own value system and its limitations.

Buying Fear Reliever 2: Help Them Expand Their Own Self-Belief System

All of us have our own self-belief system – that imaginary world inside of which we feel safe, comfortable, and satisfied. Anytime we start to do something that violates our world, we feel as though we are on dangerous ground, and we become afraid to try things our emotions have not allowed us to experience before.

Help your applicants overcome such fears by enabling them to reevaluate their own self-belief systems. One way to do is to help them focus on how great the benefits of joining your branch of service will make them feel. Another method is to help them fully understand what becoming a member of your branch of service will be like.

Buying Fear Reliever 3: Assure Them of the Wisdom of Their Choices

Some people are so self-confident they don't hesitate to buy anything they want or need. However, those people are few and far between, and for most people, buying, or in your case, committing, is an unsettling experience.

A thousand questions may be rushing through an applicant's mind as he or she contemplates a decision to commit: Is this the right thing for me to do? What will so-and-so think about my decision? Can I handle the lifestyle change? Is military service really for me? Do I really need the benefits my recruiter is promising me?

You can do applicants a big favor, and boost your chances for gaining an accession, by reassuring them of the wisdom of their decision. Of course you can't tell them they are doing the right thing, any more than you can tell them that not committing is the wrong thing for them to do. You are not a judge and you don't have to be. What you can do, however, is reassure them they are making a wise decision – at least from a values perspective. Here are some ways you can do that.

First, you have to believe in the military recruiting opportunity yourself. Military service provides many wonderful opportunities, but it's not for everyone. If you know in your heart that a decision to commit is not wise for a person, you are not much of a professional if you try to convince him or her otherwise. But if you know it's a wise decision, reassure that applicant with all your persuasive power.

Second, recap the benefits to show them how wise the decision is. You'll be amazed how often a major benefit dawns on an applicant only after the fifth or sixth time you repeat it. Don't assume he or she understands each benefit; make sure they do.

Third, reinforce all the applicant's positive feelings about committing. If an applicant expresses a liking for some benefit, get him or her to talk more about it. If an applicant is silent, ask what he or she likes most about what you've shown. Give your applicant an opportunity to take psychological possession by asking what he or she is looking forward to the most. The more your applicants are talking positively about the benefits you've shown, the more they are convincing themselves.

Fourth, answer any questions your applicants may have. Honesty is the best policy throughout the recruiting process, but both honesty and complete openness are an absolute must during the Convince Step. Stop everything you are doing and ask if they have any questions. Now, not later, is the time to find out if there are objections and what they are. In the next step, we'll share some insights on how to handle objections. And one thing you certainly never do is take objections lightly. Deal with them as they come up or they will act like earmuffs to block out everything you say.

One caution: if you ask for questions, then appear to hedge on an answer, you could destroy all the convincing you've done during this all-important step.

Checklist for Chapter 10

☐   When people believe in something enough, they'll take action on it.
☐   It makes little difference what you believe is true; you must be able to back it up with proof your applicant will accept.
☐   Applicants expect recruiters to make claims for what they offer, but they are most impressed when someone else makes or endorses those claims.
☐   As trust in you and confidence in the value of your offer rises, fear of committing disappears.
☐   Four actions you can take to set the stage for your applicants to commit:
   1.   Prove your claims.
   2.   Bring your own witnesses.
   3.   Justify the commitment.
   4.   Relieve the applicant's fear of committing.
☐   There are five ways to prove every claim you make:
   1.   Never make a claim you can't back up with facts.
   2.   If you can prove it, show your evidence.
   3.   Reinforce all claims visually.
   4.   Let applicants experience it themselves.
   5.   Repeat important claims and proofs again and again.
☐   Four ways to bring witnesses to your applicant:
   1.   Try to get a written endorsement from every satisfied accession – ask for it.

2. Carefully select the endorsements you use.
3. Treat endorsements with dignity and respect.
4. Try to involve happy applicants or accessions with your new applicants.

☐ Three ways to relieve your applicant's fear of committing:
1. Reconcile the commitment decision with their value system.
2. Help them expand their own self-belief system.
3. Assure them of the wisdom of their choices.

Chapter 11
The Tie It Up Step: Concluding and Closing

Tie It Up: Asking the applicant to commit, negotiating agreement, finalizing, re-inforcing and then cementing the commitment. It is also servicing your applicants and accessions in ways that guarantee strong referrals and an ongoing, productive relationship.

Tie Up the Sale, Not the Applicant

We believe closing a sale is not about using clever gimmicks to trick people into doing something they really don't want to do. In fact, closing is not the center-piece of the IMPACT Selling process, around which all other elements are built. Rather, tying up the sale is the natural outgrowth of doing the other five steps well. It's an orderly step taken deliberately at the end of a series of actions. Fur-thermore, it can be fun – both for you and for the applicant.

Remember: people want what you are offering or they wouldn't have agreed to meet with you in the first place. In fact, they probably wanted some of the ben-efits your service can offer before you personally entered the scene. Perhaps they didn't even know everything they wanted until you showed them what your op-portunities could do for them. Maybe you did such a good job that you convinced them to join your branch of service instead of accepting another opportunity. At any rate, you cannot build a successful recruiting career by roping today's alert applicants into accepting opportunities they really don't want.

Therefore, if they want it and you want to offer it, it's a simple process of tying up the loose ends of the transaction. As with each of the steps, there are proven procedures you can follow.

Negotiate the Conditions of the Commitment

Successful negotiating is working out an agreement that's satisfactory for both parties. It's also handling the details so everybody wins.

In a way, everything you have done up to now has been a part of negotiating the commitment. For example, if you've followed the IMPACT Selling System, you have already done the following:

1. Investigated to discover who was most interested in your recruiting opportunities.
2. Met with qualified prospects to enter into dialogue on your offerings.
3. Probed to find out what they wanted most and under what conditions they would commit to getting it.
4. Applied your most appropriate solutions to their most compelling needs and desires.
5. Convinced them you can solve their problems and fulfill their wishes by committing to your recommendations.

That's the informal part of negotiating; without it you cannot enter into formal negotiations. If you skip over any one of those five steps, you will sabotage your own best efforts to tie up the sale.

If you have completed those five steps, you are ready to start the formal negotiating process. Here are some winning strategies to help you.

Open the Negotiations on a Positive Note

A great time to begin the formal negotiations is right after your applicant has expressed approval or delight over some feature or benefit. You simply ask, "*Is there anything that would keep you from going ahead with this?*" Then STOP! This is the most useful question ever devised for opening up any negotiation. It's a sincere and honest question; it cuts to the heart of the matter, and it is not offensive in any way. However, the key to asking it properly is to stop after you've asked it and wait for the applicant to respond. The question says it all. Be sure to listen very carefully to what the applicant says. If he or she says, "*No!*" or "*I don't see any reason not to join*," you can assume the sale and begin taking care of the details. Very often, however, the applicant will show some hesitancy and offer some reason for not going ahead. If so, don't panic; just go to the next strategy.

Get All the Conditions and Objections on the Table

Applicants rarely say, *"I'll join under the following conditions."* More often their response will take the form of *"I don't know! That's a lot of years to have to serve!"* or *"I would prefer a different career field."* Expect this sort of answer, and don't be shocked when it occurs, because it will. At this point, many recruiters react somewhat frantically and start hammering away at all the reasons why the career field or another issue shouldn't make a difference. And that's a big mistake!

It's a mistake because most stated conditions are only smokescreens to cover up

Is It the Lifestyle?

Sergeant Robinson was sure she'd presented a golden opportunity to Jimmy, a college senior, who was headed to medical school next year. The four-year scholarship Jimmy was being offered was worth more than $150,000. She had asked the right questions about Jimmy's goals, presented the features and benefits of the scholarship program in the correct manner and provided the names of five medical students who were having their education paid courtesy of the military.

She asked Jimmy *"Is there anything that would keep you from going ahead?"* His response was a simple, *"Yes."* She was calm, cool and in control. Robinson then asked, *"What is it that would keep you from accepting the scholarship?"* Jimmy answered, *"I'm not sure if my fiancé wants me to join. The only thing she knows about military family life is what she has seen on TV or in the movies."*

Robinson then asked, *"Is there anything other than your fiancé's concern over the family lifestyle that would cause you not to go ahead?"* Jimmy assured her that if his fiancé had a better understanding of military family life, then he would be comfortable accepting the scholarship.

Where did Sergeant Robinson make her mistake? How can she recover?

She handled and isolated the objection very well. Now, the single issue is whether she can convince Jimmy's fiancé that the military family lifestyle is something she would also enjoy.

deeper feelings of uncertainty. You simply cannot negotiate with a smokescreen; as soon as you satisfy one condition, the applicant will raise another.

Here's where you must return to the Probe Step, because the IMPACT Selling System is a closed loop system. Whenever you meet resistance, return to the Probe. That's the only way to get all the conditions on the negotiating table, so you can deal with them one at a time. Ask questions like *"Is this the only reason you'd be hesitant to join?"* or *"If we could solve that problem, could I presume you'd be ready to go ahead?"* By pursuing this line of questioning, you'll eventually bring all the conditions into the open.

Don't be afraid of this process. It's better to have negative feelings and thoughts come out than to remain unaware of what's causing your applicant to resist making a commitment. When you feel you have all the conditions on the table, you can proceed to the next strategy.

Make Sure You Understand All the Conditions

Often there is more than one reason why someone is hesitant to commit. To uncover each one, remember to ask some form of this question, *"Is that the only reason that would keep you from going ahead?"*

Make sure you understand the conditions your applicant has cited. If there are several reasons, record them and restate each one in your own words to ensure you understand each issue.

You might say *"Okay, let me see if I understand what you've told me. You feel uncertain about being able to handle the rigors of basic training, and you're concerned about giving up some of your personal freedoms. Is that right?"*

It's More Than the Lifestyle
What if Sergeant Robinson had asked, *"Is there anything that would keep you from going ahead?"* and Jimmy had answered, *"Yes,"* but then she either failed to ask what the issue was ('lifestyle') or, worse yet, didn't ask if there were other issues to consider? What if there was also a concern about Jimmy having to deploy? How about concerns over whether Jimmy could be placed in harm's way?

You need to uncover every stumbling block to gaining the commitment and deal with each one separately.

It's important that you understand exactly what your applicant feels and demands. It's equally important for the applicant to recognize that you know what he or she is feeling. And the only way you can reach that kind of understanding is through dialogue. For example, you may surmise that an applicant is worried, "*I can't do this,*" but what the person is actually worried about may be "*I don't want my friends to make fun of me if I don't make it through basic training.*" There is a big difference between those two positions. Continue the dialogue until you are confident you and the applicant agree on what the stated conditions mean.

Offer to Try to Work out Any Problems

At this point, make it clear to your applicant that both of you are sitting on the same side of the negotiating table. In effect, you're saying, "*I know you'd like to have the benefits I've shown you, but I also know you have some concerns. I want to help you deal with those concerns, so you can enjoy the value of the benefits you want.*" To do this, you'll simply agree with your applicant, and offer to help him or her work out any problem.

It's important to come out of the first strategy with a clear understanding of every condition under which your applicant will commit and maintain a trust level that shows you're interested in providing exactly what he or she wants.

Clear Away Objections

Objections are the remaining conditions you must deal with before an applicant will agree to commit. Furthermore, the way you handle objections will often determine whether or not you gain the accession.

Almost always, an applicant will raise an objection from a feeling rather than a factual standpoint. In practice, this means you need to deal with all objections by addressing the true feelings behind them. The recruiter who responds flippantly to an objection about the length of the enlistment contract by saying, "*The time will pass faster than you think; besides, look at all the money we're going to give you for college!*" is only asking for trouble.

The reason some recruiters deal so poorly with objections is they don't know how to respond properly. Too often their training focused on learning canned responses for every objection that could possibly come up. They sound like a recorded message: "*If the applicant gives objection number four, you answer with response number 67.*" That approach is just plain wrong.

Simplify the Objection

At least half the work of solving any problem is stating the problem clearly and succinctly. In fact, when the recruiter restates the objection in the form of a question and asks that question in terms the applicant can understand and reflect upon, the objection often disappears.

It's not always easy, but it sure helps for you to know exactly what that applicant is feeling. That's what you achieve when you break an objection down to its simplest form and state it as a question.

It's All in the Question

Some recruiters like to rephrase an objection back to the applicant in the form of a question. For example, *"What I hear you saying is that you don't want to commit to any basic training dates that would prevent you from attending your brother's wedding? Is that correct?"* Or *"What I understand you to mean is that you're not sure you want to enlist for more than four years of active duty. Is that right?"*

Questions help the applicant clarify the objection in his or her own mind. It's not unusual for an applicant to hear the recruiter paraphrase the objection and realize that it isn't as big an issue to resolve as he or she thought.

Make Sure They Understand All the Benefits

Never assume an applicant understands all the benefits you've explained just because you've covered them once or twice. Make sure your applicant fully understands them. Go over them again and again.

Test to See the Objection Is Gone

Amateurs brush aside objections with canned responses. After sweeping them under the rug, they proceed as if there were no conflicts in the applicant's mind. When the applicant walks out the door without making a commitment, they can't understand why.

By contrast, smart recruiters always test to make sure they've handled each objection to the applicant's satisfaction. They verify it is gone and won't come back to haunt them. After presenting the benefits, it's necessary to seek the applicant's reaction: *"Does that answer your concern?"*

Sergeant Trenton and His Opportunities

Sergeant Trenton learned this lesson the hard way. He recruits for a reserve component. His recruiting offerings include bonuses for enlisting in certain career fields, cross-training opportunities and the chance for most of his applicants to keep the same rank they held when they separated from active duty. Whenever he met with applicants, he would recite the list of benefits he could offer.

When he lost one particular applicant to another service branch, he asked the person why he chose the other opportunity. The answer confused him: "*I liked the fact I wouldn't have to go through basic training again.*" Trenton was shocked. He assumed his applicant already knew he wouldn't have to repeat basic training, so he never brought up the subject.

Whose fault was that? You guessed it; it was Trenton's fault. His applicant never got the picture, because Trenton never made it clear enough. It was plain to Sergeant Trenton, but not obvious to the person who counted the most – his applicant.

It's a simple test, but it does two important things. First, it lets you know if the objection is gone. If it's still there, you can ask what concern the applicant still has and get more specific with your response. Second, it provides the applicant an opportunity to verbalize his or her own way of dealing with the objection. You'll be surprised how often applicants will pick right up on it. "*Sure, I remember my cousin saying he was worried about joining for six years, but he also said he would never have completed his college degree while he was in the service if he hadn't had joined for that long in the first place.*"

Now you're ready for the next big step.

Assuming the Sale

Everything you've done up to this point is wasted motion – unless you get the applicant to commit. However, that's not as big of a deal as many recruiters make it out to be. If you have carefully followed the first five steps – found out what your applicants want most, shown them how they can get it, and negotiated all the conditions necessary to gain agreement – you have every right to assume the applicant will agree to commit.

Assuming the sale is statistically the most effective, proven way to gain commitment. And while you can't make the decisions for your applicants, you can facilitate the decision-making process for them. Let's look at two ways to approach some time tested, proven techniques for making the commitment decision easier.

Pose a Question

When you feel the time is right, come right out and ask for the commitment. Ask questions like *"What day would you like to enlist?"* Or *"Would you like to get started on your application for a commission?"* However, the way you ask the applicant to join can make it either easy or difficult for the applicant to make a decision.

Think about some of the feedback questions you have been using. *"Does everything look okay?"* or *"Is there anything that would keep you from going ahead with this?"* Those questions are letting you know if your recommendations have been on target. If the responses are positive, you're in great shape. If not, don't ask for the commitment yet. Instead, return to the Probe Step. There is nothing tricky about it. You don't need tricks, if you've done a good job of following the selling process.

Asking for the commitment is merely a matter of tying up the loose ends of the transaction. You look your applicant straight in the eye, and ask him or her to commit! Don't say another word until your applicant has responded.

Many recruiters are so afraid of rejection they feel they must break any silence that lasts more than a few seconds. They may even jump in and say something illogical like *"Now I don't want to make you feel pressured"* or *"Maybe you want more time to think about this."* All that does is delay the decision and perhaps permanently destroy your effort. Try to remember that some people just need a little space when they're making a decision.

Make a Statement

Some recruiters prefer not to pose a question to gain the commitment. Instead, they assume the applicant wants to commit, and the effort to gain commitment takes the form of a statement. Here are two examples: *"Let's get you set up for an enlistment ceremony,"* or *"Let me show you how to get started."*

With this approach, applicants don't have to make one big decision to commit, just a series of little decisions, and many applicants feel much more comfortable with that method. One the other hand, when you issue a statement, applicants who are not ready to commit may feel pressured and offer up some objections. If that happens, lay the paperwork aside, and return to the Probe step to find out why they are hesitant.

Deal With Fear of Making a Decision

Often you will find an applicant is sold on the recruiting opportunity and feels comfortable with all the conditions of the commitment, but is simply hesitant to say "*Yes*" to joining.

Don't Rush the Applicant!

Petty Officer Paulson's applicant stopped him and said, "*Look! If you can give me a few minutes to think about this, I might say yes. If you have to know right now, the answer is no!*"

"*Take as much time as you like!*" Paulson said, with a great big smile. He pushed the enlistment paperwork aside and talked to the applicant for 20 minutes about her family's concerns. When they were done talking, the applicant signed the paperwork without a moment's hesitation.

If you sense your applicant needs more time or space to make a decision, probe into why he or she is hesitant. If you discover a key issue, try to settle it just as you would handle any objection, and go on with the transaction.

Usually, it helps to focus on that key issue by returning to the Probe step. Do that by asking a question. For example: "*If it weren't for the reporting date, would you be ready to go ahead with this opportunity?*"

If the applicant says "*Yes,*" then you know exactly what you are dealing with and can try to negotiate new conditions he or she could accept. If not, keep probing until you pin down that one key factor and deal with it.

Reinforce and Cement the Sale

Once an applicant decides to commit, many recruiters think they should rush through the paperwork and get him or her out of the office as fast as possible, before the person changes their mind. That's a big mistake!

If applicants want to back out, they'll find a way to back out – no matter what they've agreed to do in your office. What's more, your haste to get them out the door can damage the trust bond you've worked so hard to create. It's better to take a few minutes to tie up some loose ends before they leave.

We recommend reinforcing the sale with any of several strategies.

Compliment Your Applicant on His or Her Choice

Saying *"I think you've made a great choice"* is a simple and effective way to reinforce an applicant's decision to commit. It not only congratulates the applicant, it also opens the door to express positive feelings about the decision. The more your applicants talk about the choices they made, the more comfortable they will become with the idea of joining.

This self-acknowledgment can help head off several problems. For example, if someone your applicant respects questions the decision later, your applicant will be confident enough in their choice so as not to be talked out of it.

It's Not Just the Features and Benefits
Sergeant Lorenson recruits nurses. She is very careful about making the right recommendations that address each applicant's situation.

Once she gains commitment, she congratulates her applicants on having made the right choice. And she goes even further by reminding her applicants about how they will enjoy all the specific benefits they were most interested in receiving. Whatever made her service branch the right option for her applicants is what she stresses, and she applauds them for accepting the opportunity.

How can you do the same thing with your applicants?

Assure Your Applicant of Satisfaction

Advise your applicants they are not alone after they decide to commit. Just promise, *"I'll check back with you next week to see if you have any additional questions."* Or *"I'll be following your paperwork through the system to ensure you get everything we promised you."* Furthermore, in an appropriate situation, you could say *"If your spouse (or parents) would like to stop by with you and talk to me too, I'll be happy to answer all their questions."*

Anytime you promise to contact your applicants, make sure you do. If there is a problem and you don't check back, you'll damage the level of trust you previously established.

It's All About Service

Now the hard part starts. You've gained the commitment, and your new job is to deliver even more service. You must ensure whatever you promised is delivered precisely the way you promised it would be. To do anything less is to abandon your position as a recruiting professional and shortchange your applicant.

Don't be tempted to walk away and hope your applicants will be happy. The only way to guarantee their satisfaction and ensure they will follow through on their commitments to join is for you to monitor the activities that go along with their processing. And if problems do occur along the way, don't be tempted to use an excuse like "*I have no control over how they treat you at the processing station.*" To your applicants, every person in a military uniform, or every civil servant they have to deal with, is an extension of you, and they expect the same professional level of treatment. If that doesn't happen, you need to acknowledge and apologize for the incident, and bring the problem to the attention of the organization at fault.

Always remember, there's another good reason for providing outstanding service. Not only does it ensure your applicants receive what you've promised them, it also gives you the opportunity to maximize your relationship for obtaining productive referrals. And speaking of referrals, there's often disagreement among military recruiters about when to ask for them. We believe you should only ask for referrals when you have earned the right to do so. With some applicants, it could be when they find out they have been booked into the job they want, or it could be after they graduate basic training or technical training school. It's up to you to determine when the time is right. Some recruiters and supervisors of recruiters think it's a good idea to start 'perpetuating' right from the first appointment. We don't agree. Think about your own experience when you were considering joining the military. Before you were absolutely sure the recruiter and branch of service were going to deliver on every promise, did you feel like volunteering the names of several of your friends? How about when you consider making a major purchase such as a house, car or large appliance? Do you like being asked to provide referrals before you know if the salesperson or product is going to perform the way you would like?

Never forget that part of your job is to develop your applicants to the point they become active spokespeople for you and your branch of service. There's no better way of gaining more accessions and developing raving fans for you than by providing outstanding service after your applicant has agreed to commit.

Recruiting duty requires a lot of hard, diligent work. However, there's not a more important job in the military. But if you can't finalize transactions, you'll never succeed at recruiting. It's all about helping your applicants take ownership of the recruiting opportunity.

Checklist for Chapter 11

☐ Tie It Up: Asking the applicant to commit, negotiating agreement, finalizing, reinforcing and then cementing the commitment. It is also servicing your applicants and accessions in ways that guarantee strong referrals and an ongoing, productive relationship.

☐ The Tie It Up Step is not the centerpiece of the IMPACT Selling System. It's a natural outgrowth of doing the five previous steps correctly.

☐ Successful negotiating is working out an agreement that's satisfactory for both parties.

☐ Open up the formal negotiations right after your applicant has expressed approval or delight over some feature or benefit. Ask, "*Is there anything that would keep you from going ahead with this?*" Then STOP!

☐ Objections are the remaining conditions you must deal with before a commitment can be secured. Be sure you get every objection on the table, and resolve them one-by-one by returning to the Probe Step. The way you handle objections will often determine whether or not you gain the accession.

☐ Don't assume an applicant understands all the benefits you've explained. Go over them again and again.

☐ Make sure you understand all the conditions under which the applicant will commit. This includes such conditions as career field, departure date, rank, etc.

☐ When you feel the time is right, ask for the commitment by posing a question such as "*What day would you like to enlist?*"

☐ If you prefer not to pose a question, simply assume the applicant wants to commit, and offer a statement like "*Let's get the paperwork started.*"

☐ If you sense your applicant needs more time or space to make a decision, probe into why the applicant is hesitant and treat the situation like you would any objection and move on. However, don't pressure your applicant; it could destroy all the trust you have built to this point.

☐ After you gain the commitment, reinforce the decision to commit and provide outstanding follow-up service.

☐ The time to ask for referrals is after you've earned the right to do so.

Chapter 12
How to Build and Sustain Momentum

We believe success breeds motivation, not the other way around, because it's extremely difficult to become motivated if you're experiencing failure after failure. However, why do some people seem to always be optimistic and enthusiastic about what they do, no matter what the short-term outcome?

Motivation, Resilience, and Optimism

First, let's look at two realities.

- You are responsible for your own motivation, resilience, and optimism.
- You are responsible and accountable for your own production numbers and performance.

Don't ever believe it's someone else's responsibility to make you successful. It doesn't work that way. You must create your own success.

Motivation: The drive to perform.
Resilience: The capacity to rebound from setbacks or difficulties.
Optimism: The belief that positive outcomes will be the result of your actions.

Successful recruiters share some common traits.

- They have strong product knowledge, and they accurately apply it to address an applicant's needs or solve an applicant's problems.
- They have strong selling skills that give them confidence to perform at high levels.
- They have the capacity to be optimistic, resilient, and optimistic in the face of any obstacle.
- They have the physical stamina and resolution to work as long and as hard as necessary to succeed.
- They enjoy recruiting duty, take pleasure in seeing themselves in the role of military recruiter and are fueled by the rewards the profession provides them.

The 10 Most Essential Success Truths in Military Recruiting

We profess that success as a recruiter starts on the inside. And here are the 10 most essential success truths we believe are critical to your recruiting career.

1. **Success is progressive and gradual.** It's never a one-time, cataclysmic event. Your recruiting accomplishments will build over time. Don't rely on one big month or one big quarter of productivity to propel you to your organization's recruiting hall of fame. Instead, realize long-term success results from working to your fullest capacity day after day. It's a series of victories that, over time, will contribute to taking you to whatever achievement level you seek.

2. **Life isn't fair.** Nobody starts out equal with anyone else. Therefore, get over it and move on.

   Stop comparing yourself with someone else. Why? Because you're not someone else. You are you – and not one other person on earth has your exact DNA, skills, or background. As a consequence, it's impossible for any group of recruiters to be on equal footing.

   Instead, start comparing yourself with your own potential. What does that mean? Great recruiters don't compare themselves with other recruiters. They don't wish they had a better territory or different supervisor. Instead, they dig in and make themselves responsible for maximizing every opportunity that comes their way.

3. **Self-discipline is the universal differentiator between highly-successful and marginally successful people.**

Sprint to the Line
Recruiting success is not a marathon race. Instead, it's a long-term series of sprints you'll run one at a time.

Successful recruiters are disciplined. Ironically, there's not a career field in the military that looks like it requires less discipline, yet actually requires more self-discipline

Top recruiters tend to win smaller victories more often. They work hard to avoid long droughts between victories. If they have a big month, they celebrate it and quickly move on to another challenge.

than recruiting. It's tempting to be as free as a bird and spend your time doing the wrong things. However, top recruiters stay on task… and they don't need any outside push to remind them they should be prospecting, making face-to-face presentations, servicing applicants or working on their professional knowledge.

4. **Successful people have in-depth wisdom and insight about their area of endeavor that others don't have.**

How much time and energy are you prepared to invest in your recruiting career? Are you willing to study, learn, and master the skills, mindsets, competencies and talent requirements that can give you the competitive edge?

Life Can Be a Total Funk
Sergeant Bradley always seemed depressed. He would have an occasional good recruiting month and then slip into a funk that lasted for weeks. He couldn't understand why Sergeant Rose kept getting more national leads. He was also upset by the contests that certainly appeared to favor his office partner, Sergeant Matthews, a recent recruiting school graduate who backfilled the top recruiter in the organization after she retired. Bradley perceived Matthews' zone as 'target-rich' and the prime reason why Matthews' applicants always seemed to accept the career fields that earned the most points in the recruiter competition system. On the other hand, Bradley was assigned his recruiting zone after his predecessor was relieved of duty for lack of production. Bradley even believed his supervisor was feeding the national leads to Rose so she would win the contests.

What was Bradley's problem? Was he jealous of Rose and Matthews? Even if he was, what good did it do him? What could he do about it?

People who are masters of their craft see patterns and relationships others don't see. They find opportunities where others see oceans of despair. They relate things others see as being unrelated. People seek them out for advice, including their prospects and applicants.

Who's Cheating Whom?

Petty Officer Sindon was a recruiter. However, she also had a side business that she operated out of her house. Because her recruiting office was close to where she lived, she often went home at lunchtime to make phone calls and fill customer orders.

Eventually Sindon started making some side-business calls from her recruiting office during regular duty hours as well as selling products to her applicants. She believed that if she delivered acceptable recruiting results, all would be fine.

What do you think about her self-discipline? What problems was it causing? How honest was Petty Officer Sindon being? What would you do if you were her supervisor and discovered that she was doing this?

5. Potential is a renewable resource that should be used, not saved for the future.

One of the worst things someone can keep telling you is *"You have great potential."* Why is that? If you're over 12 years old, it means you have ability you're not using.

Potential is a renewable resource. As you access it, you can always go back

Where Will You Be in Two Years?

Smart recruiters devour every training opportunity they can find so they can become experts in their profession. They read books, listen to audio programs, attend workshops and seek out other great recruiters to learn how they excel.

If you'll invest just a few minutes every day in product knowledge, marketplace research, improving your selling skills, personal growth, and acquiring more insight about recruiting, you'll be a recruiting expert within two years. If you don't do any of these things, in two years you'll be two years older – but your insight, knowledge and understanding about your profession will be where it is today. Is that where you want to be?

Is This as Good as it Gets?
The worst thing that ever happened to Marvin is he completed his college degree during his first six years on active duty. The tragedy to befall Ike was he graduated first in his class at recruiting school. Meagan's problem was that she was the rookie of the year her first year on production.

All three of these recruiters suffered from the very same problem: they had potential, used it and never renewed it. Do you know someone like that? Some people dwell in the past, either regretting times they can never live again or feeling totally satisfied with the success they enjoyed earlier in life.

Then there's Brad; he showed great promise as a recruiter, but never wanted to get out from behind his desk. There's Karen, who turned down a chance to get a commission because she worried she wasn't ready for the additional responsibility. And there's Nancy, whose supervisor told her she could easily be recruiter of the year if she would just work a few more hours per week. Unfortunately, Brad never left his office, Karen never re-applied for a commission, and Nancy refused to work two extra hours a week.

Which group of people is worse? Those who displayed great potential and then never renewed it or those who never used their potential in the first place? It makes no difference, because they're both in the same place – nowhere. How about you? Are you using your potential?

to your inner source and get more. As you grow and expand, that resource constantly reinvents itself and takes on a new shape, direction, and life.

6. No one will ever be any more successful than they see themselves as being.

We talked about your self-image earlier. However, the subject bears revisiting.

You will never achieve any level of meaningful success that flies in the face of the self-image you've created for yourself. Your self-image is the cumulative result of everything you have ever understood as being said, written or otherwise communicated about you. If what you've heard is positive, your self-image will be strong. However, it doesn't take very much to pollute your mind – perhaps only a negative word here or there. Unfortunately, it takes a lot more than you'd ever imagine to repair even minimal damage.

ILLUSTRATION

What Do You Call Yourself?

What is the job title on your business card? Does it say 'recruiter' or something else? We've met hundreds of recruiters over the years who use the term 'representative.'

When we ask them why they substitute representative for recruiter, they usually say it's because they think their prospects, applicants and influencers think negatively when they hear the term recruiter.

There are a few problems with their line of thinking. First, everyone who works for your branch of service, military or civilian, whether they are assigned to recruiting duty or not, is a representative of your armed service. However, they are not all recruiters. They are not assigned a production goal; they don't wear a recruiting badge; they don't get special duty assignment pay, and their career field or military occupation does not say they are a recruiter.

Second, do you really think the people you talk to can't figure out you are a recruiter? The badge on your uniform is a dead giveaway – it says recruiter – not representative. Furthermore, when one of your prospects goes home to talk to their parents, do you also think the term 'recruiter' never pops up in the conversation?

If you can't call yourself a recruiter with a satisfying smile on your face, you're in the wrong profession. Be proud of yourself, your branch of service and the fact you are a recruiter.

You can only change your self-image over time. You must develop a set of affirmations, visualize yourself being successful and then go about the business of making yourself a winner.

7.   Success is more often about listening than about talking.

We've discussed this concept throughout the book. However, it's worth revisiting – it's that important. When you do all the talking, you are just explaining things you already know. When you listen to others, you'll learn what they know. And there's a big difference.

You will have a great deal more success in any venture, whether it's recruiting duty or some other occupation, if you act more interested in other people, in learning about their ideas, philosophies or point of view.

> **Questions for You**
> - What have you enjoyed most about this book?
> - What principle or strategy have you found most applicable to your recruiting career?
> - How will you put it into practice?
> - How valuable would it be to you if you spoke with other recruiters who read this book and discussed what they enjoyed about it, the strategies they found most valuable and how they are putting the book's ideas into practice?
> - When you ask other people for their opinions or perspectives, you learn a lot more than if you do all the talking. And success is all about learning, isn't it?

Think about this for a moment. If I listen to you, I'll learn about your interests, your dislikes, your likes and your preferences. If you listen to me, and I do all the talking, I'll never learn any of those things.

8. **Don't major in minors or confuse activity with results.** You can be busy doing all the wrong things.

As a recruiter, time is your only inventory. You need to be positive you're doing the right things, at the right time, for the right reasons.

To do that, focus on the actions most essential for your success – carefully positioning yourself, prospecting, pre-call planning, being in front of qualified prospects, making effective presentations, servicing applicants, seeking referrals or productively learning more about your target markets, offerings, and recruiting skills.

It's All About Time
Sergeant Green has been in recruiting three years.

However, she is frustrated. Following a very successful rookie year, her production has dropped off the last two years. She's active in a women's softball league and basketball league, takes two college courses each semester in the evenings, goes sailing or golfing with her boyfriend on the weekends, and she is studying for her promotion exam at the same time.

What advice would you offer Sergeant Green to help increase her recruiting production?

9. **Successful people master their emotions, instead of allowing their emotions to master them.**

How good are you at 'compartmentalizing' your life? How effective are you at preventing a setback or failure in one part of your life from spilling over into another area?

A Great Way to Get into Trouble
Sergeant Richardson prided himself on his ability to gain commitment from his applicants. In fact, his colleagues gave him a fitting name, *"Bulldog."*

However, Richardson sometimes let his emotions get the best of him. One of his applicants backed out of his delayed enlistment contract and opted to join another armed service. Not being one to take something like that without a fight, he drove to the applicant's home and confronted him on the doorstep. He wanted to know why he backed out after making a commitment and demanded to know the name of the recruiter who *"stole"* him away, because he was going to make that recruiter pay for what he did. According to the applicant, Richardson became verbally abusive, so he called Richardson's supervisor to complain.

When his supervisor asked him for his side of the story, Richardson did not deny his anger and admitted he cursed out the applicant to his face. When Richardson's supervisor started to counsel him against displaying such behavior, the conversation evolved into a shouting match as Richardson accused his boss of not supporting him, especially since he was the top recruiter in the region.

Did Richardson cross the line?

Do you allow personal problems to affect your professional performance? Do you allow professional setbacks to affect your personal life?

If you allow either of these things to happen, you won't discover the success you deserve. Even a cursory look at life will tell you the most successful people in any venture are able to move past problems or obstacles and not allow them to distract or derail them from their long-term goals.

Emotions are important. They are part of who you are. However, if you allow anger, frustration or any other emotionally charged attitude to override your good sense or judgment, you'll likely regret what you did for a long time to come.

10. Successful people have heroes, and they work hard to become someone else's hero.

Who is your hero? Who is your role model? If you don't have one, find one. Ask yourself how that person would handle the difficulties, frustrations, and challenges you face in your recruiting career. Then model his or her behavior.

Here's your real challenge. Work hard to become someone else's hero. Use the ideas in this book, and we guarantee you will become someone's hero, someone's recruiting hero. And then you really will have become successful, won't you?

Checklist for Chapter 12

- ☐ You are responsible for your own motivation, resilience, and optimism.
- ☐ You are responsible and accountable for your own productivity and performance.
- ☐ Successful recruiters have common traits:
  - Strong product knowledge.
  - Strong selling skills.
  - Motivation, resiliency and optimism.
  - Physical stamina.
  - They enjoy being a recruiter
- ☐ The 10 essential success truths in military recruiting:
  1. Success is progressive and gradual.
  2. Life isn't fair.
  3. Self-discipline is the universal differentiator between highly successful and marginally successful people.
  4. Successful people have in-depth wisdom and insight about their area of endeavor that others don't have.
  5. Potential is a renewable resource that should be used, not saved for the future.
  6. No one will ever be any more successful than they see themselves as being.
  7. Success is more often about listening than about talking.
  8. Don't major in minors or confuse activity with results.
  9. Successful people master their emotions, instead of allowing their emotions to master them.
  10. Successful people have heroes and they work hard to become someone else's hero.

Index